Pen to Paper

Dedicated to all those who work or have worked at Newhaven's Pen Factory.

Malcolm Troak

Malcolm Troak

New Anzac Publications.

By the same Author;
We Will Remember Them
Peacehaven's Old Tin School
Two Years and an Early Breakfast
Peacehaven and Telscombe, Then and Now

This paperback edition published in 2005 by
NEW ANZAC PUBLICATIONS
30 Central Avenue,
Telscombe Cliffs,
East Sussex BN10 7LY

ISBN 0-9539115-4-3

Front Cover: *A Black Parker Mk 1 Duofold Centennial Fountain Pen.*
Designed and manufactured in Newhaven to commemorate the
100th Anniversary of the Parker Pen Co. 1888 / 1988.

Designed and Typeset by EH Graphics (01273) 515523. East Sussex.
Printed by Pageturn Ltd (01273 821500). East Sussex

Contents

Introduction

This book has been written in response to a great many requests from ex Newhaven Pen Factory personnel who fear the early and indeed even the more recent years, have never been recorded and consequently will be lost for ever.

As I discovered during my own research, memories of the early 1920s, when the site was first established by Felix Macauley, are very difficult to find.

Hopefully however this book will serve to allay some of those fears and at least capture many of those still available memories and anecdotes and commit them to paper.

As Winston Churchill so famously said " A nation that forgets its past has no future".

This, therefore, is not a book which deals specifically about writing instruments (there are many excellent books available which deal with this subject). It is, however, a story which traces the operation of the Newhaven Pen Factory from its infant days in 1921, when it was little more than a few wooden huts, to the current time, where it is probably the largest state of the art quality pen factory on one site anywhere in the world.

Of course, Pens, Pencils, Ballpens and Accessories are covered but specifically those products which were designed and manufactured within the Newhaven Factory.

The operation of the factory through various owners, Managers, Directors and, of course, the very dedicated and extremely knowledgeable workforce forms a large part of the script.

Personal anecdotes and stories have been included to add the all important human and sometimes humorous touch to the narrative.

Finally, it has been said many times that "one picture is worth a thousand words", so for that reason a great many images have been included in this book.

Malcolm Troak, Telscombe Cliffs

Acknowledgements

Without Pony Eager's power of persuasion this book would probably have never been written. Pony convinced me of the need and gave me great support with his wonderful memories of the early days, so thank you Pony.

I would also like to place on record my sincere thanks to both David Ruderman and Francis Benham of Parker Pen Newhaven for supplying me so many copies and photographs in my quest for information.

Christa Brailsford and all the girls at Le Bureau at the Needlemakers, Lewes for their wonderful clerical support.

Peter Bailey and his voluntary crew at the Newhaven Local and Maritime Museum for their input and many copy photographs.

Also all those ex Pen Factory workers, far too many to name individually, who gave me so many wonderful stories and loaned me some delightful photographs. Unfortunately in a book of this nature it has not been possible to include them all, but if someone would like to write a second volume!!!

Finally all my family for their encouragement and guidance during the long hours of research and leaning over the laptop.

Thank you all.

"No man was more foolish when he had not a Pen in his hand or more wise than when he had".

Samuel Johnson.

CHAPTER 1
Felix Macauley - *"The Felix Works"*

Almost three years after the end of the First World War a certain Felix Macauley submitted plans to the Newhaven Urban District Council in East Sussex. These plans were for the conversion of a number of redundant ex-Army Huts into a Pen Factory, to be called "The Felix Works" which consisted of Felix Macauley Ltd and Gold Nibs Ltd.

From this small beginning commenced a chain of events which would see these few wooden and corrugated iron huts over time transform into the largest and most modern quality writing instrument factory anywhere in the world.

This then is the story of that transformation and the people, products and events which made those changes possible.

This picture shows the First World War Transit Camp on which the Parker Pen Factory is sited. Little did these smart soldiers of the Bedfordshire Regiment know that some of their wooden huts would be converted into the first Pen Factory. The picture is dated 24th July 1918.

Newhaven, East Sussex 1921

During the First World War the port of Newhaven on the River Ouse, and the local Railway had played a major part in transporting men and materials across to France.

To accommodate those men awaiting transportation across the Channel to France, a hutted transit camp was constructed on a large flat piece of ground on the Eastside of Newhaven.

The camp was fronted by Railway Road which gave direct access to both the Docks and the Railway.

At the end of hostilities in 1918 the transit camp was used for a short time as a rehabilitation area for troops returning from the Front. It then became redundant and most of the huts were either removed legally or illegally by the locals, who made their own garden sheds, etc. from the reclaimed material!

Enter Felix Macauley

Unfortunately little is known about the man Felix Macauley or his previous background. It has been suggested that he had at one time worked for MacNiven and Cameron's, who were a small fountain pen manufacturer in Edinburgh, but that has never been substantiated.

However, whatever the circumstances, either Felix Macauley or one of his Managers knew a great deal about fountain pen manufacture and, perhaps more significantly, the "art" of making quality gold fountain pen nibs.

A site plan submitted to the Newhaven Urban District Council on August, 21st 1921 detailed alterations and additions to buildings for conversion to Works, Railway Road hutments - the first Pen Factory.

A letter accompanied the site plan which said:"I should be pleased if you will kindly submit the attached plans for the approval of the Urban District Council of Newhaven and shall be glad if this matter can be expedited at the earliest possible date." The letter was signed by Oscar Drew Harris, Works Manager.

Ten days later, on August 31st, 1921 the planning application was

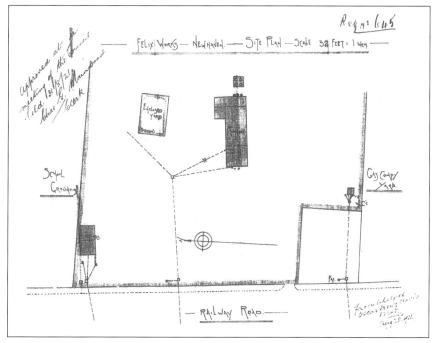

This plan shows the original application by Felix Macauley to convert some of the old Army huts into Pen Factory Buildings. The plan is dated 28th August 1921.

approved; it was in today's terms certainly "fast-track".

The site in Railway Road had a frontage of 288 feet (87.7 metres) which gave tremendous scope for any future development.

On the north side the boundary was the Harbour Infants School built in 1895 (and still standing) and to the south the Newhaven Town Gasworks which "straddled" both sides of Railway Road.

To the rear of the site there was a very large earth embankment which had been constructed to prevent any flood waters from the River Ouse encroaching on the main A259 Coast Road. The Eastside area was at that time very prone to flooding.

Alterations and additions to the old Army Huts consisted of a small two room office, a main factory building which comprised:

    - Grinding Room - Turnery - Polishing Room

    - An Engine Room to house the Crossley gas engine to drive all

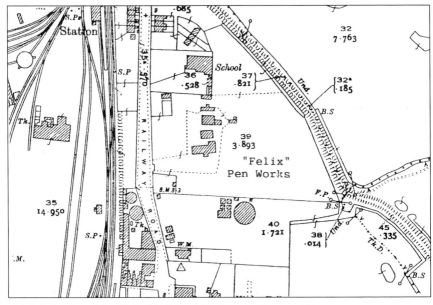

A 1928 site plan of the "Felix Works", which shows just how small it was.

the equipment from a central shaft.

- Two small internal W.Cs for females, and

- finally in the far south corner a corrugated iron W.C. for the men.

From the list of manufacturing facilities it can be seen that the factory would have been equipped to produce pen parts from day one.

The opening of a factory on the Eastside of Newhaven would have been greatly welcomed by the whole Newhaven community and particularly any female workers.

Factories had never been actively encouraged by the local council, even with a growing population in 1921 of 6,829.

The major employers in the locality at that time were

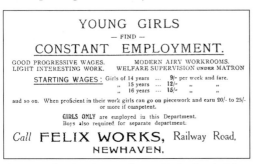

A very early advertisement for specifically female labour requested by Felix Macauley. The wages quoted would probably have been considered reasonable for the mid 1920s.

the Port and Docks, the Railways and Marine Workshops and a small Fishing Fleet, and these were of course predominantly male jobs.

If one was really desperate they might have tried the Tarpaulin Works or, worse still, the Silica Works where flint beach pebbles were crushed to make abrasive powder. All but two of the original employees were to die of lung disease!

Adjacent to the Felix Works was the closely knit community of Eastside - the east side of the River Ouse - who have always maintained a separate identity to Newhaven Town. Eastside is particularly proud of its nickname "Turkey Town". The name apparently came from the time when live poultry was imported from Normandy and unloaded on the Eastern Dockside. Aromas of roasting turkeys, which had somehow disappeared from the docks, used to pervade Eastside!! This was an ideal catchment area for recruitment to the new factory, particularly for female staff.

Many of those early workers were to remain making pens and pen parts for all their working lives and, in many cases, completed over forty years of service with Felix Macauley, Valentine and Parker Pen. It was not

Or if not the Felix Works how about the Newhaven Tarpaulin Works in the tall sheet sheds. It certainly appears to be a most awkward position in which to work!

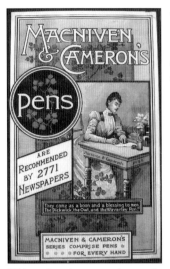

This advertisement shows the company, Macniven and Cameron's where it has been suggested that Felix Macauley learnt his trade.

unknown for their children and even grandchildren to follow in their footsteps.

Jack King, for example, joined Felix Macauley in 1923, the year that they were officially incorporated as a company. His first job was as an office boy working for the head of the business, Mr Sigmund Wade, but he quickly realised that the workbench appealed more than an office desk. He, therefore, became a five-year indentured apprentice in the Gold Nib Shop, which was the most important department in the factory and demanding the most skills. He became Nib Shop Foreman, Works Manager, Director, Managing Director and finished up as Chairman of the Parker Pen U.K. Board, completing a grand total of over 60 years service.

By all accounts, working conditions were far from ideal within the Felix Works; however, despite that, all the workforce appeared to be quite a contented group of workers.

A very good account of life under Felix Macauly has been left by Cyril Ireland, a born and bred Newhavener, who in his time also worked for Valentine and Parker Pen.

Felix Macauley - by Cyril Ireland

A friend who worked at the Felix Macauley pen factory at Newhaven told him that a job was open there. Seeing the chance of higher earnings, Cyril went along and was lucky enough to be taken on at 10/- a week (50p). He was 14 years old and considered these good wages for those days.

Fitting bands. His first instructor in the ways of pen making was Mr Fred Bailey. Cyril's first task was the cutting and fitting of rolled gold bands to pen caps. The bands, thin rings of metal, were cut to the correct size from tubes of rolled gold, placed in position by hand and then hammered in a collet - a metal flange which applied pressure and forced the band into a tight fit around the cap.

Then he was transferred to hand-turning of pen barrels by shaping and drilling rods on a lathe and, once again, Fred Bailey taught him the mechanics of the job. At that time all the pens were made from the hard rubber substance called Vulcanite. Later came a material called *Erinoid* which was made from sour milk and other unlikely ingredients. *Celluloid*, a plastic substance made from camphor and cellulose nitrate, also came

Eva Blaber who joined Felix Macaulay at the tender age of 14 in 1922. She became a first class nib slitter spending all her working life at the pen factory.

into use for making components but it was a highly inflammable material. Cyril recalls one day that a batch of components was going through the process of shrinking in a special oven, when the lot caught fire and caused quite a scare.

Rough place. Conditions generally were very rough in almost every respect - machinery, facilities for staff and the very buildings themselves. These were converted wooden huts which had been used by the Army during the first World War, and were sited on bare earth, which in wet weather became a quagmire.

Despite the bleak surroundings, Cyril remembers those days as being very happy. At one period there was a craze for making long cigarette holders by screwing thin rods of vulcanite together and boring a hole through them. There were many ostentatious cigarette holders in use at the factory for a while - some of them 18 inches long!

Although lots of variously named pens were made by Felix Macauley to be sold by other companies as their own brands, Cyril remembers that they all seemed basically the same design, with only slight variations of

The method shown is the way that the Hard Pellet was welded to the gold nib blank in the 1920s. Compared to the method used today it looks archaic to say the least!

This is the old fashioned method of slitting gold nibs. Even the most experienced operators carried scars on their fingers where the nib had slipped and the revolving disc had cut the unprotected fingers.

shape. They either had a simple eye-dropper filling system or a lever filling system. The Company developed a large export trade in pens for the Indian market and when, for some reason, Bible classes in India became fewer, the market fell away and Felix Macauley was forced to cut some of their staff.

Another worker, Tom Winton, remembers how he was taught to fashion pen caps and barrels on a very old-fashioned belt driven lathe.

Later he was trained to assemble completed caps and barrels, having to ensure both components fitted together properly. As both caps and barrels were hand-turned, there was inevitably a slight variation between components, so the final assembly involved an alteration being made to the thread inside the cap in order to give a perfect fit on the barrel. Thus each pen acquired a certain individuality because no other cap would fit it perfectly!!

Tom was paid 18 shillings (90p) per week for this work, of which 15 shillings (75p) went on board and lodgings to Mrs Mercer of Eastside.

Factory Extensions

A few Planning Applications were submitted during the mid 1920s to either extend the premises or improve working conditions.

This is the only known photograph of the Felix Macauley workforce, probably taken around 1925. Charlie Lower can be seen first left, centre row, and a very young Jack King second right, centre row.

For example, in 1925 a very small Dining Hall and Ablutions Area were built. This was to enable the workforce to eat their sandwiches, etc. in a separate area away from their machines.

In 1926 a small "add on" outhouse was constructed to form a laboratory and, finally, in 1929 what was proudly described as a "boiler house" of brick construction was also added.

The size of this boiler house was 6' x 6' (1.8 x 1.8 metres) so the boiler could not have been much larger than a domestic type coke boiler!

This was the extent of the building changes by Felix Macauley which were not really significant but, as we shall learn, "from small Acorns great Oaks will grow".

Fountain Pen Manufacture

Based on information gleaned from various people who had worked for Felix Macauley, it is quite apparent that the work was distinctly labour intensive. Very little investment was

Cyril Ireland who worked for Felix Macauley, Valentine and Parker Pen. He left an interesting summary of his working life making pens and pipes.

made in updating the original pen making equipment so that everything appeared to be done by hand, even to welding the hard pellet to the gold nib blank.

It really was a "jobbing shop" operation, with the Management fully prepared to manufacture complete fountain pens or just component parts for other well known pen makers.

As we have learnt from Cyril Ireland, there was an export business to India but that collapsed when Indian Bible classes reduced!

Ellen Zanetti who was one of the first office workers to join Felix Macauley when he established his pen factory. She worked in the factory offices all her working life retiring after forty two years of service.

One story, which has been handed down from ex Felix Macauley workers, is with regard to nib gold being "pawned" to pay the wages, particularly during the worst of the depression between 1921-31.

The raw gold was held in a local bank at Newhaven. If money was in short supply to pay the wages, an arrangement was made with the Bank to "pawn" sufficient gold to pay the outstanding wages! When the cash flow improved, the 'pawned" gold would be re-purchased.

There was also some attempt to involve the workers in a few out-of-work social activities, the most memorable apparently being the coach trip to the British Empire Exhibition which was staged at Wembley in 1924. This must have been a truly fascinating experience for the whole workforce, as many of them would not have previously travelled far away from their home town.

The End of an Era

With the depression in the late twenties and thirties continuing to affect all industries, it was no surprise to find that Felix Macauley, like so many companies, had to reduce his workforce.

U.K. based pen manufacturers also reduced their dependence on such

1924 and two Southdown Charabancs take Felix Macauley's workers on an outing to the British Empire Exhibition. This was held at Wembley on the site which would eventually become the famous Wembley Stadium.

contractors and brought the work back "in house", which would also have affected companies such as Felix Macauley.

It was probably fortuitous that at this particular point in time Mr Harben James Valentine, Managing Director of a private company called *Valentine and Son, Photographic Publishers* was looking to extend his pen manufacturing base.

As he already had the Valentine Pen Factory (originally Gillard Willett and Co. Ltd.) based in the City of London, it is possible that he was aware of the Felix Macauley Works, either through the Trade Press or through the supply of pen component parts out of Newhaven. However, whatever the circumstances, an offer was made, accepted and Valentine and Sons became sole owners of the Felix Works, Newhaven in 1930, which consisted of Felix Macauley Ltd and Gold Nibs Ltd.

The workforce of Felix Macauley must have been very pleased with the end result because they were all retained and had increased continuity of work in a difficult period for manufacturing.

Harben Valentine must also have been satisfied with his investment. Not only did he increase his fountain pen manufacturing capacity but, more importantly, a highly motivated and skilled workforce, particularly with regard to the manufacture of high quality gold fountain pen nibs.

He had also acquired a large open site, which would allow extensive development to accommodate any future growth plans for his business.

This is a view of what lay in store for Felix Macauley's workers when they arrived at Wembley. The American style roller coaster must have appeared like something from another planet and the various exhibition pavilions from around the British Empire equally mind blowing.

CHAPTER 2

The Valentine Pen Company

It was not generally known that the Valentine Pen Company could trace its "Roots" back to 1881, when James Valentine founded the very famous postcard company *J. Valentine and Co, Dundee, Scotland.*

Later on in 1900 under Managing Director Harben James Valentine (1872 - 1949) they became a private limited company describing themselves as "Photographic Publishers".

A price war with certain German postcard publishers between 1910 and 1914 had a very serious effect on the business. They decided, therefore, to diversify into Greeting Cards, Calendars, Cut-out Children's Books and "PENS".

It is known that Valentine already had a small Pen Factory in London during the 1920s and were producing a limited range of fountain pens.

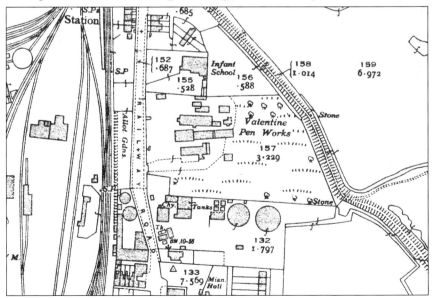

This is a 1938 plan showing the Valentine Pen Factory. The factory has grown considerably since it was taken over from Felix Macauley, however it still resembles an "out-of-line" jumble of huts!

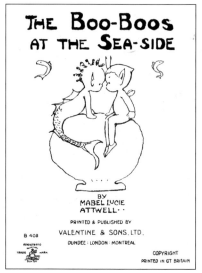

THE **Boo-Boos**
AT THE **Sea-side**

BY
MABEL LUCIE
ATTWELL

PRINTED & PUBLISHED BY
VALENTINE & SONS. LTD.
DUNDEE : LONDON · MONTREAL

B 408

COPYRIGHT
PRINTED IN GT BRITAIN

The other side of the Valentine business was the printing of books and cards. Valentine was used extensively to print and publish books for children and in particular stories by Mabel Lucy Attwell. This picture shows just that.

Therefore, when Valentine bought out Felix Macauley in 1930, they already had some experience of the writing instrument business.

The first Annual Return of the Valentine Pen Company, Newhaven, East Sussex of July 14th, 1931 shows a nominal share capital of £51,100. Four Directors were listed on the return, of which two were shown as members of the Valentine family. These are shown below:

Valentine, Harben James - Sandforth, Fife, Printer & Publisher

Valentine, Douglas Stuart - Southdown Road, Seaford, Sussex, Fountain Pen Manufacturer

Harben Valentine continued to run the Printing Business in Dundee, whilst Douglas Valentine ran the Fountain Pen Factory in Newhaven.

One of the first Management changes to be made by Douglas Valentine was to make contact with Jack King and offer him the position of Gold Nib Shop Foreman. This was considered to be the most important production department in the factory at that time.

Jack King, a very accomplished pianist, had taken a break from Felix Macauley to set up his own professional dance band and had been away from the area for two years.

The company had specialised in the manufacture of high-quality gold pen nibs, many of which were exported to Europe and India. Jack King, who had served a lengthy apprenticeship learning the "art" of nib manufacture, knew the nib business "inside out".

Harold Franklin, who joined Valentine straight from his school in Newhaven in 1935, gives a very vivid description of what it was like to work in the pen factory stores during the mid 1930s.

The mid 1930s and the management and office staff of Valentine all have their photograph taken.

Harold Franklin

When he joined the Valentine Pen Company, which operated on what is now the Parker Pen factory site, he started work as a Stores Ledger Clerk and had come straight from school to his first job. By the standards we know today at Newhaven, the conditions left a lot to be desired, but to young Harold they just seemed normal. Even now looking back he says: *'for those days in 1935 the Valentine factory wasn't too bad. I don't think other factories were much better, so we didn't feel we had cause to complain".*

At that time only about 100 people worked for Valentine, few enough for everyone to know everybody else and Harold, having been born in Newhaven and educated there, knew many of the people anyway. So he settled down to his new surroundings quickly, despite the fact that the factory consisted of large wooden huts and that coats were hung in a tin shed and were nearly always damp when put on again after a few hours. During wet weather the ground around the huts was turned into deep mud, through which one had to slosh during the frequent journeys about the premises.

Again the mid 1930s and it's now the turn of the factory staff to have their picture taken. The Newhaven Museum at Tates Garden Centre has a copy of this photograph with a list of around 95% of the people identified.

The Valentine pens were manufactured from the best materials then available, celluloid and casein - the plastics of their day, but not to be compared with what we know as plastics nowadays.

Celluloid, a compound of camphor and cellulose nitrate, was a very highly inflammable substance, so Harold's department had to take special precautions in storing it, making sure it was well protected and isolated in its own room. Used to make the pen barrels and caps, it was delivered from the manufacturer to Valentine in the form of tubes of the correct diameters, which were then cut into appropriate lengths before final shaping and polishing.

All celluloid had to be ordered twelve months in advance of delivery as the manufacturers had to allow this period for the sheets to 'cure' or mature before it was fit to work. The sheets were then rolled into the tubes for Valentine.

Casein was used also for pen barrels. It was made from bones and milk. The third main substance in those Valentine pens was ebonite or vulcanized rubber, from which nib feeds were made.

The British pen market in the 1930s was still largely dominated by the 'big boys - Swan, Waterman and Onoto (although Parker was becoming known more and more). As far as Valentine pens were concerned, their big markets were all overseas and mainly in France and India. On occasions, when Swan were unable to keep up with production themselves, some parts were made for them by Valentines.

Harold cannot recall that there was any very famous Valentine pen. *"There were too many different models turned out, he says, "The company never concentrated on any single brand leader but would make special models for specific markets and sometimes in rather small, uneconomic lots."*

For instance, the various distributors around India each had different ideas about the pens that would suit their own particular areas and would tell Valentines to make special designs for them, often specifying all the details of shape, colour, size, nib, etc. In some cases they wanted only a few dozen of these, but Valentines always supplied them. Two names which Harold remembers, were the 'Rajah' and 'Krishna' pens.

After working for about two years in the stores, Harold was transferred to the office to work on cash ledgers and was still there when in 1941 he received his 'call up' papers.

Apart from nib manufacture, another very important operation was that of polishing all caps and barrels to give them a very highly glossed finish.

Molly Packham started work with Valentine in 1931 as a Trainee Polisher. It was considered to be quite a skilled job, as the finished product depended upon manual dexterity and a "good eye". The slightest slip of the mop could easily destroy a cap or barrel.

Molly's story of her polishing days with Valentine highlight the type of working conditions very prevalent at that time.

Mrs Molly Packham

In March 1931 Molly had come straight from school to her first job in the Valentine Pen Company. Work was not very easy to find in those days, particularly in a small community like Newhaven. So Molly considered herself very fortunate to obtain the position even though her first wages were only 7.6d (38p) a week. It seems very little now but in fact it was considered fairly good then for a young girl.

Molly remembers that she was given a thick denim overall, almost as stiff as canvas, with buttons up the back.

"I am sure they wore just the same clothes in prisons" says Molly. To complete the old-fashioned factory worker appearance, she also had to wear an elasticated mop cap.

Her work was to polish pen components on a rotating wheel. This wheel, like all the other machines in those wooden huts, was powered by a driving-belt from a rotating shaft in the ceiling.

The metal wheel had a covering of soft padding onto which a very strange mixture had to be placed in order to polish the pen parts. It was made from a substance called *rotton-stone*, which is de-composed siliceous limestone and wax. Molly remembers that the rotten-stone, which looked rather like dried lumps of mud, arrived from Germany in large barrels and before use had to be soaked overnight in water. The

The operators in this photograph are using revolving mops to hand polish pen caps and barrels. It was a very skilled but dirty job where the operators used yards of sticky tape to protect their fingers from the mop. This method was used until the 1950s when rotary dial polishers were introduced.

It looks almost Dickensian but believe it or not this was the original nib shop. Nib making was a very skilled job and called for extraordinary manual dexterity.

resulting wet mud was then smeared on the buffs and wax applied on top. When the pen component was held against the spinning wheel it imparted a dull polish to the rough surface. Afterwards the part was then glossed on a plain buff wheel without any rotton-stone mixture.

Record family. Molly's family must surely hold the record for the number of their people working at the Newhaven factory. No less than nine of them were working there at the same time just before the war - seven sisters and two brothers, and up to the war they had a total of 150 years service between them!

Building Work

Several small additions were made to the factory during 1932, but nothing of any real significance until July 1934 when Oxley and Bennett, a reputable local builder, commenced work on the site.

A large extension was added to the Turning Shop and the Assembly Department also increased in size.

These extensions and additions served to double the size of the manufacturing unit from that purchased from Felix Macauley. However, it still remained a "Hotch Potch" of various shaped buildings, all with different roof heights and not even built parallel to one another.

The biggest complaint from the workforce was still with regard to the muddy access route to the factory and between the various departments, as no pathways had been laid.

Apparently Mr Valentine, Director in charge of the factory, was considered to be a very good boss to work for. Cyril Ireland remembered him regularly going around the factory and talking to the men and women at their benches and machines. He was always sympathetic to any grievances and put things right when he could.

One of the foremen, who had responsibility for plastics' production, was Charlie Lower. He spent all his working life in pen manufacture at Newhaven and trained many hundreds of people on the various machine operations.

Joan Weiss, who joined Valentine at the tender age of fifteen, remembers him well.

Mrs Joan Weiss

As school days finished she went to her first job working as a servant in a farm house near Piddinghoe, but very soon realised that she would not be able to stay long as the work was hard and the atmosphere not very friendly. So, hearing that there were vacancies in the pen factory at Newhaven, then owned by Valentines, she applied for work and was taken on by Mr. Charlie Lower, Foreman. She was 15 years old.

She worked in one of the old huts which then comprised the Newhaven factory and which stood on rough, unpaved ground. The girls wore long, thick cotton overalls and old-fashioned mop caps. They worked in bleak conditions, at machines which were powered by leather belts running up to a drive shaft under the roof. Joan's job was the grinding

A typical Valentine Fountain Pen of the late 1930s.

Jack King MBE. It was Jack King who trained so many operators in the skills of pen nib manufacture. A firm disciplinarian but absolutely fair, he insisted the workforce both worked and played hard.

of nib feeds to shape - 36 feeds being done in each operation on a large grinding wheel.

She says that she will never forget Charlie Lower, who impressed her as being a real 'character'. A small man, with a head of long, wild black hair and what appeared to be a severe cast in one eye which looked sideways!

He invariably addressed every girl as 'Mary' even though he knew each one's name perfectly well. The result was hilarious, for none of the girls ever knew to which of them he was speaking.

As well as making their own brand of fountain pen, Valentine were prepared to also carry out subcontract work for other pen makers. These included Swan and Waterman, who regularly used the facilities of the Valentine "chasing machine" to engrave the very fine patterned lines on their hard black rubber caps and barrels. This, however, 'dried up' with the introduction of multi coloured caps and barrels when engraving was no longer needed to "enhance" the outside surface of the pens.

Some investment had been made in more modern machine tools, particularly in the turning section. Small Capstan type lathes had been purchased as well as very accurate Micron Centre lathes. This investment certainly improved the "threading" of components when it became no longer necessary to 'match' caps to barrels - a considerable quality improvement and a real saving in terms of labour and time.

An American manufactured machine was also purchased, which was specifically designed to grind the front end of the Ebonite pen feed to the correct shape every time - thirty six at a time. This totally eliminated the need to continue with the laborious and inaccurate method of shaping feeds by hand.

The fountain pens produced by Valentine were equal in terms of quality and performance to other U.K. brands, such as Onoto, Conway Stewart, Swan and Wyvern.

Valentine concentrated on plastic products with very little enhancement, apart from a few different styles of bands around the cap. In fact, the majority of U.K. produced pens during this period looked very similar in shape and style, with ink filling either by a side mounted lever or a "push button" under a blind cap at the end of the barrel.

A common fault with most fountain pens, including Valentine, at this time was with regard to the rubber sac used as a reservoir inside the pen barrel to hold the ink. This was very prone to perishing and was a constant cause of complaint.

So the Valentine Pen Company limped along, giving work to over a hundred local people but lacking both a large sales force and a strong cash flow, they were never going to pose a real threat to any of the larger pen makers.

However, there was an unscheduled but very significant change about to take place when war clouds loomed and war was eventually declared on 3rd September 1939.

The Valentine Pen Factory as it was in 1939. It still resembles a few single storey huts and sheds and certainly no parking problems with only one car belonging to Jack King.

CHAPTER 3

The War Years 1939-45

Parker Pen Arrive

Just prior to the outbreak of the Second World War, Jack King had been promoted to the position of Works Manager with responsibility for the whole of the Valentine site at Newhaven, reporting directly to the General Manager, Jack Grundy.

In later years he was to describe this as one of his most satisfying achievements and a job he undertook with the utmost relish.

However, it did prevent him achieving one of his other ambitions, which was to join the RAF at the outbreak of war. The job of Works Manager was classified as a "Reserved Occupation" and as such he was to remain at the factory for the duration of the war. To make it worse his General Manager, Jack Grundy, was accepted into the RAF! !

Almost from day one of the commencement of hostilities Ministry of Defence Inspectors came down to the factory and assigned specific metal components to be made on site. These included firing pins and precision torpedo parts manufactured to very close tolerances and very high volumes in collaboration with the Petroleum Research Unit. This necessitated an immediate switch to running the factory for twenty four hours a day on a three shift system, for six days a week, using both male and female staff.

New skills had to be quickly learnt as the materials supplied for the various components were made from different types of steel and totally dissimilar to the plastics and metals used in pen manufacture.

Special cutting tools, gauges and detailed drawings were supplied by the MOD who had their own inspectors on site to ensure approved quality levels were maintained.

A canteen had to be organised to cater for the three shift working. Air raid shelters around the factory grounds had to be arranged and also fire watching schedules for the night-time.

These two gentlemen had the foresight to see the opportunity of "taking an interest" in Valentine in 1941. The man on the left being Mr Zoccola, Managing Director of Parker Pen UK and on the right his Chairman, Viscount Molesworth. Both these men had boundless energy and drive putting Parker Pen firmly on the map in the UK.

On top of all this many of the men and women were either "called up" to serve in the Forces or were moved to factories around the country to help manufacture munitions.

Fortunately Jack King had managed to have several of his key workers, such as setters, classed as "Reserved Occupation", but nonetheless there was an enormous amount of training for both new and existing staff in a very short space of time.

Some pens were still being made, albeit under very trying conditions and a major shortage of materials. With most of the machinery converted to munitions work, only 20% of normal pen production was being achieved.

Then in 1941 Parker Pen UK came on the scene!!

It was in December 1941 that the UK Parker Pen Company, which was a wholly owned subsidiary of the American parent company, acquired an interest in the Valentine Pen Factory, Newhaven.

A Trust Deed for securing Valentine stock amounting to £27,000 was signed on 2nd December 1941 by Ronald Leng Harben for Valentine and Frederick William Dilnott for Parker Pen.

Mr Dilnott was a Director and Secretary of the Parker Pen Co, London and for the remainder of the War he and Jack King virtually ran the factory with little or no interference from anybody from the Valentine family.

Parker Pen in the U.K.

As background to the reason for Parker Pen UK acquiring an interest in the Valentine Pen Company, it is necessary to understand how the Parker Pen operation evolved in the U.K. and Europe.

This picture shows the Parker Pen Canadian Factory in Toronto. It first supplied component parts for assembly into Parker products at Newhaven during the war years.

Writing instruments, supplied by the American Parker Pen factory, had been on sale in the U.K. since at least 1899. An advertisement of December 23rd, 1899 clearly shows premises at 195 Oxford Street, London with a large Parker Pen sign on the outside of the building.

Subsequently in 1922 George Parker decided to carry out a tour of the European Countries to establish for himself the export potential.

Based on his findings he decided to set up a wholly owned distribution subsidiary in London during 1924.

He had already had a factory equipped in Toronto, Canada during 1923 to supply 60% of its production output to the U.K., for both the domestic and export markets within the rest of Europe.

A Distribution Centre and Sales Office were established in Norfolk Street, London and run by an American, Mr Korst. Unfortunately Mr Korst did not fully appreciate or understand the European method of selling writing instruments and in the first year the U.K. company lost the equivalent of 100,000 US Dollars.

Mr Korst returned to the USA in May 1925 and was immediately replaced as Managing Director by Mr Alexander Raphael Zoccola who, as an ex Parker Pen Salesman in South America and South Africa, set about changing the U.K. business operation.

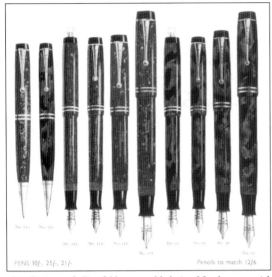

PENS 30/-, 25/-, 21/-   Pencils to match 12/6

A selection of Duofolds assembled in Newhaven with Canadian made plastic components. Some of the nibs are from Newhaven production.

One of the first things he did was to obtain much more prestigious offices at Bush House in The Strand. This also gave him extra space, which eventually enabled him to bring in component parts from the Canadian Factory and assemble them "in house" with considerable savings in costs.

Mr Zoccola was an extremely astute business man, who understood how to sell to the public and was quite prepared to take on a market that was at that time dominated by pen companies such as Waterman, Swan and Onoto. He can certainly be credited with putting Parker firmly on the map in the U.K. and later Europe.

The War comes to London

When the Second World War came along, staff at the London office were at their highest level of over one hundred and Parker Pen products were being sold and distributed to both Europe and parts of the Commonwealth.

Then, without any warning, Parker Pen were instructed by the Government that they would have to vacate Bush House as the basement was required for special BBC operations.

With very little time allowed the offices and workshops were "evacuated" to 15 Govesnor Gardens, which at that time was in a pretty derelict state and was a labyrinth of small rooms.

In spite of the War, products and components continued to arrive from

Canada. However, one particularly large shipment of stock, which would have covered sales for nine months, was torpedoed just off the English coast near Liverpool.

Fortunately divers were able to rescue the entire stock but, of course, it was badly contaminated with sand and salt and became a mammoth cleaning operation for the whole Parker staff.

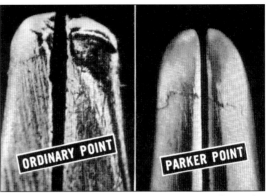

Once Newhaven commenced making gold nibs for Parker products there was a great deal more emphasis on producing to the agreed Parker quality standard. This picture was used to highlight the difference between a competitor's nib and a Parker nib.

This situation really alarmed Mr Zoccola, who quickly realised the company could rapidly run out of stock, particularly with the War in the Atlantic Ocean showing no sign of abating.

He, therefore, set about finding a suitable supplier or factory which was not a simple task, as most factories had been "requisitioned" to produce important munitions for the war effort.

Fortunately for future generations of Newhaven people and other local towns, he "found" the Valentine Pen Factory and agreed a legal arrangement where Parker Pen would "share" the Valentine Pen Company's manufacturing facilities for at least the duration of the second World War.

The Continuing War Years

Once the joint agreement was signed and sealed with Valentine, Alfred Dilnott, as Secretary and Director of the Parker Pen Co, was to spend considerable amounts of his time in Newhaven.

He was known as a particularly hard taskmaster, who was really only interested in maintaining a supply of Parker products to the marketplace. As he was the only Director on site, it was no surprise to learn that Parker utilised significant amounts of any available capacity after munitions to make pens.

The first Parker products despatched out of Newhaven had been assembled from components delivered from Canada. Duofold pen nibs were the first Parker parts actually produced in Newhaven. Apparently none of the nib making equipment had been assigned for munitions manufacture, hence the readily available capacity.

The nibs were stamped with the letter "N" to identify them as Newhaven production, as against those produced in America or Canada.

Eventually, over time, caps, barrels and the other Duofold components were made in Newhaven.

One significant difference between the Canadian and the Newhaven model was that the nib section was a screw fit to the barrel, whereas the model from Canada had a "push fit".

The one Parker product made solely in the Newhaven factory was the Parker Victory Pen.

Although the factory received no direct hits from enemy bombers this one on September 10th 1940 was too close for comfort! Two high explosive bombs were dropped on this electricity power station which was just opposite the factory's air raid shelter. No real damage was done to the factory except a few broken windows and loss of electricity.

On Tuesday 22nd November 1944 a barge loaded with 180 tons of high explosive blew up under the Newhaven cliffs. It took out all of the factory windows and several of the roofs were ripped off. The picture is of Newhaven Harbour Station just down the road from the factory.

The First Khaki Duofold

The first Parker pens Tupps Strudwick remembers coming to the factory were khaki coloured Duofolds. The components were imported from Canada and assembled at the Newhaven factory. The standards of assembly for Parker were set so much higher than the operators were used to, that for a long time they were very nervous of the Parker work. Miss Strudwick well remembers one of the inspectors being so meticulous in examining Duofolds that, instead of the normal 500 Valentine pens a day, she passed only 130 Duofold!

Owing to severe material shortages in the U.K. several Duofold and Victory models were made using different colour caps and barrels, but such was the demand for Fountain pens that any product sold as soon as it got into the shops.

Jack King was certainly the manufacturing powerhouse during the war. His enthusiasm was indefatigable. As well as the long hours at work he also virtually ran the local Home Guard, and made sure most of the male workers attended the weekly drill nights and reported for guard duties!

Edie Feist and Sheila Harvey who both worked on shift work producing munitions during the Second World War.

"Dig For Victory" was highly publicised as a way of helping the War effort. Jack, therefore, had allotments opened up in the factory grounds for anyone who wanted to grow their own vegetables.

Tom Evans, who joined Valentine just before the War as a fourteen year old and spent all his working life with Valentine and Parker, had this to say about his experiences:

It was on April 1, 1939 when Tom, then aged 14, joined the factory straight from school as an Operator.

Barely a year out of school, young Tom Evans lied about his age, joined the Home Guard and spent his nights patrolling Southease Bridge near Newhaven. Come the dawn and it was back to Newhaven and the Valentine Pen Company to begin work on the early shift making striker pins for land mines.

With the outbreak of war, spare time was soon something of a luxury, so you'd think a spot of gardening would be low on his list of priorities. Not a bit - as part of the Dig For Victory campaign, all Valentine employees were offered an allotment on spare ground around the factory.

"Mine was where the H block is", said Tom. "We had some lovely vegetables from that allotment".

Meanwhile, the Battle of Britain was being fought in the skies by the RAF during the summer of 1940. Down below Tom and his workmates raised a hearty cheer when a plane was shot down, the pilot parachuting to safety.

"It wasn't until after the plane crashed along New Road that we realised it was one of ours!"

At the time Tom was living in Fort Road - a restricted area - and had to show a special permit every time he entered or left the street. "In the run up to D-Day we were kept awake night and day as tanks, lorries and troops streamed down to the harbour to embark on the ships."

During those dark days of the Second World War the factory worked round the clock making weapon components, although pen production continued on a limited basis.

Although the Newhaven factory did not suffer any actual bomb damage, one particular incident does stick very vividly in the minds of the night shift on Tuesday, November 22, 1944.

It was nearly 5 a.m. and the night shift was looking forward to "clocking off" when one of the largest explosions to occur in England during the Second World War hit Newhaven. All of the factory windows were blown in and several of the roofs ripped off.

It transpired that a barge loaded with 180 tons of high explosives broke its towline and drifted ashore, just under the cliffs at Newhaven Fort.

The barge then struck a mine on the beach and exploded in a blast which was felt ten miles away. Fortunately the high cliff face prevented a disaster, although hundreds of homes and business properties in Newhaven suffered damage.

Jack King immediately took charge of the situation at the factory. He was to recount later that the only materials available for repair were heavy tarpaulin sheets which were slung over the bare roofs, and tree trunks were used as weights to hold them in place.

He was pleased to report that the factory was operational and continued to produce munitions without too much delay.

With the end of the War in 1945 it was time for the UK Parker Pen Directors to decide their future direction in terms of Pen manufacture - and they didn't take long to make their proposals known to the American parent company.

This group who don't appear to be all that happy worked together in the plastics area. Taken around 1945 they are, from left to right, Jimmy Eager, John Rowe, Molly Packham, Cyril Prior and Bob Nightingale.

The end of hostilities in 1945 signalled a very significant "Wind of change" throughout the whole of the UK Parker Pen Company organisation.

First of all, with the full agreement of the American Parent Company, Parker Pen UK completed the purchase of the Valentine Pen factory at Newhaven. Newhaven employees found themselves officially on the Parker payroll and with Jack King still very much in charge as Works Manager.

The change of ownership was a very popular one at the factory for it promised a brighter future for everyone, and as the workforce had been making and assembling Parker products for over four years, they already considered themselves Parker people.

The other very significant change in 1945 was the appointment of Mr Norman Byford to the position of Managing Director of the UK company.

Mr Zoccola who, as the previous Managing Director, had done so much to establish Parker Pen as a major force in the market place, had decided to retire to his native South Africa.

This is the man who built the Parker Pen Empire, George Safford Parker. His philosophy was simple "make a better product and the public will buy it".

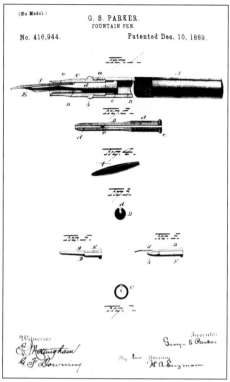

One of George Parkers patents of 1889.

He was to say before he departed: "The growth of the Parker Pen Company in the UK from virtual obscurity to a position of leadership in a short span of years, is a triumph of progressive endeavour, sound merchandising and tenacity of purpose". It was Mr Zoccola's drive and marketing strategies which had lead Parker to this position.

Before the Second World War Mr Byford had headed up a consortium of I.C.I. and Du Pont in Brazil and had been responsible for the running of five factories, so he had an established track record.

During the war he had served with the RAF Intelligence as a Flight Officer.

Returning to Brazil during 1945 he met Kenneth Parker who was visiting Brazil in an attempt to establish ink manufacturing facilities for Parker Pen.

A firm friendship developed between the two men and, aware of Mr Zoccola's imminent departure, Kenneth Parker offered Norman Byford the opportunity of taking over the role of Managing Director Parker Pen UK.

The brief apparently given to Mr Byford was simply to:

(A) Increase European manufacturing capacity to meet future sales demand.

(B) Promote and increase export sales of Parker products across Europe.

As we shall see, under Mr Byford's leadership, in succeeding years

Parker Pen grew in manufacturing capacity and prosperity, not only in the U.K. but also in Europe, where he developed all the Parker business which was ultimately so successful.

Meanwhile back at the Newhaven factory things were getting back to as near normal as possible after the end of the war and, of course, with the final "take over" of the Valentine Pen Company.

Although Parker Pen owned the entire site, it was still managed under the name *The Valentine Pen Co.* for administration purposes. In fact, employees' wage packets still bore the name Valentine until 1957 when everything was changed completely to the Parker Pen Co. Ltd.

BRITISH HOME OF THE LUCKY CURVE.
neter FOUNTAIN PEN.
to the YALE OBSERVATORY STANDARD,
ns, please apply to the British Offices of
195, Oxford Street, London, W.

This advertisement of December 1899 clearly shows the British offices of Parker Pen Co, Oxford Street, London.

Many things which had been instituted during the war years were still in place. For example the twice daily BBC radio broadcast of lively music "Music while you work" continued which was apparently much appreciated by the workforce.

Also Johnnie Latter (the original Arkwright!), who had been employed by Jack King as an errand boy, was still pedalling his Tradesman's Bike and collecting shopping in Newhaven for employees.

This facility had been arranged during the war years to assist in particular women on shift work, who could find all the shops closed at the end of their shift.

Men and women were returning to the factory after completing their wartime spell in either the Forces or in other munitions factories, so

A typical advert showing the famous "Lucky Curve" pen.

there was no shortage of workers.

Herbie Hollands returned with a D.S.M. (Distinguished Service Medal). During the war as a Corporal in the Royal Marines he was awarded the D.S.M. for his part in an attack on a German radar station in the Greek island of Milos.

Tragically Herbie was knocked off his cycle and killed on his way to work at Parkers in April 1977.

The fuel shortage and emergency of 1946 hit the Parker Pen Company very hard. No power was available to operate the machines which mostly worked from belts turned by an overhead shaft. So instead of making pens, the operators were set to work painting and cleaning the premises just to keep them busy.

One day Mr King noticed a tractor working in one of the farms nearby and had the brilliant idea of adapting one to work the factory machines. A tractor was hired from a neighbouring farmer and Harold Smith, the Chief Engineer, quickly adapted it by rigging up a belt driven by the tractor in through one of the workshop windows and thus to the machines. It worked so well that four others were obtained, also six cement mixers. With this motley collection of noisy monsters production was soon back in full swing.

However, a different source of power was needed to work the pump for the hot water system. The problem was solved by connecting the water pump to an ordinary push bike on which several boys took turns at pedalling like mad to pump water to the workshops.

Several of the operators also helped by fitting their cycle dynamos adjacent to the individual machine belt drive to produce a localised source of lighting.

Necessity was certainly the Mother of Invention in those dark days.

The '51' Pen

When the Parker '51' pen was introduced to the American public in 1941 it caused an instant sensation. Everybody wanted one!

It was given the best possible worldwide publicity by American troops who took it and showed it off all around the world.

When eventually very limited supplies became available in British shops, they sold themselves and, because they were so badly wanted, a 'Black Market' quickly developed.

Such was the European demand for this new technologically advanced fountain pen, that Norman Byford was instructed by the American parent company to have a '51' pen manufacturing capability established in Newhaven - as quickly as possible.

Coming just after the war this was easier said than done. There was not only a real shortage of raw materials, but also specialised machine tools

The factory from Railway Road in 1945. To the left can be seen the company air raid shelter which was turned into a storage area when the war ended.

and equipment, plus a need for increased manufacturing space.

In order for Jack King, as Factory Manager, to understand the '51' pen manufacturing process, the unprecedented step was taken for him to be sent to Janesville in Wisconsin, home of the American Parker Pen factory.

It was no eight hours flight to Chicago in those days! When Jack King left in June 1946 it was five days on board ship, one day by train from New York to Chicago and half a day from Chicago to Janesville. The only consolation, as he was to point out in later years, was that there was no jet lag!

He never tired of relating just how far advanced the parent company was in terms of manufacturing capability and the wide range of machine tools available from stock in the USA.

When he was eventually shown the very large obsolete machine store, he thought he had discovered Aladdin's Cave. He was allowed to select whatever equipment he wanted and this was eventually shipped to Newhaven to enable manufacture of the '51' Vacumatic to commence.

In spite of very strict building controls in place at that time, the local authorities gave approval on 29.10.46 for a new workshop to be built on

1946 and the fuel shortages necessitated agricultural tractors being used to drive the overhead shafts which in turn allowed the machines to operate. And still only one car!

A nice view of the factory taken from the top of the gasholder around 1948. The factory had been "tidied" up as a group from the parent company in America was due to visit Newhaven. The long white building towards the top of the picture is the first factory building authorised after the war. It was called the "New Shop".

the north side of the factory. This was called the "New Shop", a title which was used for many years. It housed the Autos, Capstans and Centreless grinding machines, equipment which produced caps, shells, barrels and even metal turned parts for fountain pens, etc.

Cyril Green, who was eventually responsible for all assembly operations in Newhaven, remembers how the first '51' pens were assembled from component sets supplied out of Canada.

In the autumn of 1947, just three months after Cyril joined Parker Pen, the Parker '51 ' came to Newhaven. Another wooden hut (they were large, substantial structures in which 20 to 30 people could work) was acquired in Estate Road - it had just been vacated by the Auxiliary Fire Service - and was devoted to the assembly of the new pens.

The parts were imported from the Canadian factory. A Chief Inspector from Canada started the assembly lines and trained the twenty or so operators and chargehands until they were proficient.

Everybody in Parker regarded the '51' pen as something really fabulous. It was an entirely new concept in pen design, a startling difference from the war-time Victory pen which they had recently been making.

The capstan lathe section. No sitting down allowed, payment was related to performance with piece work rates, and no work, no pay!

Reg Aldridge operating a new Cincinnati Centreless Grinder which generated the final outside shape to plastic caps and barrels prior to finish polishing.

Herbie (Sandy) Hollands who returned from the war with a DSM having served with the Royal Marines. He was tragically killed in an accident whilst riding his cycle to work.

The '51' assembly team had to acquire a much higher degree of precision in their work than had ever been necessary before."

Manufacture of the '51' Pen

With the 'New Shop' built and the American equipment installed, component production commenced during 1947. It was by all accounts a considerable learning curve. Barrels and shells were manufactured from a new American material called Lucite, which required different machining techniques to all previously used materials. The wall sections of the components were also thinner than anything previously produced, in fact they were described by many of the machinists as being 'Egg Shell Thin".

Producing the stainless steel cap, with a Lustraloy finish plus a polished band, taxed to the full the ingenuity of both the handful of engineers, setters and operators - but they did it.

Two specialists who were recruited in 1948 helped to move the 51 Pen project forward at a much faster pace.

David Clements was recruited as the one and only Development Engineer on site at that time, and one of his first actions was to set up a Drawing Office. His other responsibility was to bring 'in house' any '51' pen components made by outside subcontractors and ensure equipment was installed in Newhaven to accommodate this work.

The other was Monty Lane, who had previously run his own engineering workshop in Dover, and was an expert in automatic screw machine cam and tool design. As the '51' pen components were heavily dependent on the autos for their manufacture, Monty was the ideal person to run this section. With innovative design he was able to cut cycle times by as much as a third on many of the key components.

Season's Greetings

TO ALL MEMBERS OF THE PARKER PEN FAMILY IN
ENGLAND FROM ALL OF US HERE IN THE STATES

After the war Christmas cards like this were sent to Parker Pen workers in Newhaven from the Janesville workforce. Accompanying the Christmas cards were food parcels which were described by the recipients as "absolutely marvellous" a very welcome gift and much appreciated.

In fact, the auto shop was held up as a shining example by Browne & Sharpe and CVA who had supplied the machines and who could never understand how their machines could operate at such speeds!

Space in Newhaven was still very much at a premium and when in 1948 Jack King was told to examine the possibility of manufacturing Quink on site, he knew that he would have to locate extra premises for this to be done.

In the first instance a small shed in the grounds was set up by Ernest Woodcock, who was the Company Chemist, as an experimental workshop in order to produce trial batches of Quink. To assist him he recruited Jim Fitzgerald in June 1948.

The trials were a success but it was very quickly realised that there was no available factory space in Newhaven which would be able to accommodate an ink making, bottling and packaging facility.

An empty factory site was eventually located on the Eastern Docks, Dover. It was leased to Parker Pen and in August 1948 work started on setting up a Quink Line.

At the same time the decision was also taken to relocate all pen assembly and inspection operations into the Dover factory from Newhaven and release more space for '51' pen manufacture.

Fred Bailey, Cyril Green and Harold Franklin were transferred to Dover to set up the assembly department and to train the new operators. They were eventually to remain in Dover until 1952 when the assembly of Pens was transferred back to Newhaven!

Although the purpose of this book is to deal specifically with the

Newhaven site, Dover was always considered an "extension" of the Newhaven Factory, and for that reason a separate chapter will be written on the Dover Factory which was operational from 1948-68.

The Dymchurch Outings

It would be very remiss to finish this chapter without mentioning the memorable outings to the Beach Holiday Camp at Dymchurch in Kent during the late forties. They were still talked about by those who attended for years afterwards.

The outings were the brainchild of Jack King who realised that after the deprivation of the Second World War people needed a "lift". He was

The Newhaven workforce line-up for the obligatory photograph before setting off on their outing to Dymchurch in 1948.

The fully laden coaches head off down the Drove towards Dymchurch and the Beach Holiday Camp.

The girls tug-of-war competition underway.

also aware that with the opening of the Dover factory that there were now three separate entities in the UK operation, London Office, Newhaven and Dover factories.

His idea was for these three units to get together and to get to know each other in a social and sporting atmosphere - today the specialists would call this *Bonding*.

Coaches would set out from the three locations and meet up at the Holiday Camp for the day.

The centre for the day's activities was the Holiday Camp, which provided chalet facilities for changing and a large hall for refreshments and dancing.

Various competitive events, such as Tug Of War, Egg & Spoon races, etc., were organized between the three locations with the winners receiving a trophy to be held for one year.

The day would finish with a grand dance and then the coaches home - apparently by the vast numbers who attended - memorable days!

Even most senior management attended and participated in the activities.

And to the winners "The Parka Pen Challenge Cup". It was painted the most lurid yellow and the winners had to drink from it!

A typical English '51' display case.

The price shown on the '51' pen is 105 shillings, or in today's terms £5.25. This would have been the equivalent of over two weeks wages for the working man in 1948.

Queen Mary attends the launch of the '51' in London.

CHAPTER 5
The Fifties

The 1950s was a decade of extensive building works on the Newhaven site, and also a time which saw many significant management changes.

In terms of product requirements, the most fundamental introduction was without any doubt the Parker Ballpen Refill. This was to have far reaching effects on the Parker brand as Ballpens started to outsell the conventional Fountain Pen.

Jack King described this period as "Noteworthy for the production of the famous '51'Pen - one of the great designs in Parker's history - and for the introduction of the Parker Ballpen in 1955. These were the watersheds in years of consistent development".

New Building Works

In 1950 approval was given for the construction of a General Office and a Works Canteen.

This was followed in 1951 by the first major factory building which was always called Bays 1 - 9 and was on the south side of the site. Constructed of basically war-time materials and of "saw tooth" design, it was made up of nine separate bays. Poorly insulated and a constant source of water leaks and draughts, it none the less lasted for forty years before demolition.

When the general office was completed, it was very soon realised that it was not going to be large enough to accommodate the administration staff, which were needed to service the rapidly growing business. Therefore, in 1955, a solid brick built office complex was constructed on the site where the war time allotments had been so carefully tended.

The construction was in the form of a large 'H' which is, of course, where the term "H-Block" was derived. It was eventually converted into the shape of a conventional square building.

This aerial photograph of around 1952 shows the factory in the centre with the infant's school on the left and the gasworks on the right. The proximity to the River Ouse can be appreciated from this view.

In the first general office was housed the master clock. This clock controlled all the 'Clocking-in' points and starting, finishing and tea break bells in the various departments.

A time-keeping bonus was in operation. In order to receive the monthly bonus it was necessary to 'clock in' on time and never be late.

It was a constant battle for some of the operators to 'clock in' just before one was clocked in as late, and lost the bonus for that month.

One girl, who wishes to remain anonymous, said "I ran all the way from the top of the town to clock in, but as I put my card in I was too late! Bang went that month's bonus. I went into my department completely out of breath, took off my coat, and was immediately asked by the Foreman 'where have you been?' Without more ado, I put my coat back on and left - I didn't like the Foreman anyway - and hated having to clock in!!"

51 Aerometric

Newhaven changed over to the manufacture of the '51' Aerometric in April 1950. One of the main features was a one piece barrel as the filling method had been completely redesigned. Instead of the complicated button filler under the "blind cap" as designed for the Vacumatic, a separate revolutionary squeeze type filler unit was used.

Newhaven produced the Aerometric in four colours, with either a Lustraloy cap or Rolled Gold cap. All initial production of the Rolled Gold cap model was for "export only" and generated significant business for Parker Pen.

Component production was carried out on a piece-work basis. This was fairly straightforward at that time because the majority of operations were "operator controlled".

Pony Eager operated one of the lathes producing '51' pen parts during the early 1950s.

He remembers that all parts were loaded onto peg trays which held 155 parts - termed a *Parker Gross* - a real gross being 144!

The work study standard was calculated on a standard gross of 144, you produced 155 but were paid for 144!

The toolroom situated in Bay 1-2 in 1955. Notice particularly the toolmakers benches mounted on brick pillars.

Although the factory was owned by Parker Pen the social club still called itself "The Valentine Sports and Social Club". This happy group were obviously enjoying their first Annual Dinner in 1952.

THE VALENTINE
SPORTS & SOCIAL CLUB

FIRST

Annual Dinner

SAVOY CINEMA RESTAURANT, BRIGHTON
FRIDAY, OCTOBER 10th, 1952

"Now may good digestion wait on appetite,
and health on both."

Menu

Creme of Tomato

Roast Chicken
Garnished with Ham, Tomato

Pomme Rissolie
Garden Peas

Fresh Fruit Melba

Coffee

"Happy have we met, happy have we been,
Happy may we part, and happy meet again."

Mike Wilkinson (Wilky) was the Work Study Engineer who, with his stop watch, would establish how many could be produced in an hour. Any components produced above Wilky's hourly rate earned a bonus.

Many of the operators were very skilled at their particular job and could make it look as though they were going "flat out" when in fact they were holding back. In fact, it was not unknown for some of the faster operators to have "hours to spare" at the end of the week and had to disappear for a couple of hours.

The Control Clerk

Before the age of computers, the Control Clerk was the centre of all activity in the various production departments. It was a very important job as all work, etc. had to be checked in and confirmed by the Control Clerk.

Lorna Napper was a Control Clerk for many years and she described her work role as:

I was responsible for checking in and recording all partly finished components, which came into my section from other parts of the factory, and also for passing work to the section operators who would process the components on their machines. For instance, an operator would collect a new batch of nib feeds which he (or she) would trim and finish on a machine. Lorna recorded the number of components in the batch and also the time of collection. These details were also written on to a Daily Work Sheet for the operator. When the batch was finished, the time at completion and the number done was once more recorded. All the work that passes through the section is thus accounted for, with

Act One: Scene One

Time for Play at Newhaven

Play: *Blithe Spirit.*

Cast: *Some of the members of the plastics and moulding departments at Newhaven.*

Time: *Just before lunch on the last working day before Christmas.*

The caption tells its own story.

an accurate time check for each job. When during the day an operator exceeds the work quota, he or she then qualifies for bonus pay, which is calculated in the Accounts Department from the Daily Work Sheets kept by Lorna.

The Christmas Bonus

In the 1950s there was an annual "ex gratia" Christmas bonus paid to all Newhaven staff.

As it was paid so regularly many of the girls would order goods for Christmas at the local shops and arrange to pay for the goods with their Christmas Bonus. It all worked very well until one year when there was nothing posted on the factory notice boards to say a bonus would be paid.

Panic set in, both in the local shops and the factory, the rumour was that no bonus would be paid in that particular year!

What had happened apparently was that one of the Directors in the London office had been away and omitted to make the authorisation.

*The Annual Children's Party held in the canteen. Connie Wilkes can be seen collecting the empty plates. Locally the Parker Pen Christmas Party was **the** one to attend, and was eagerly awaited by all the children of the workforce.*

Four Toolroom Apprentices admiring somebody's efforts on a press tool. The four are: Bob Lindfield, Doug Brocklesby, Graham (Tim) Harrison and Graham Kingswood, who all turned out to be very skilled tradesmen.

The bonus payment was, of course, confirmed and payment made just in time for Christmas.

Another thing, which the staff had all agreed to do, was to work two Saturday mornings in November in order to have Christmas Eve as a holiday. In the 1950s the Christmas holiday consisted of only Christmas Day and Boxing Day. New Years Day was a normal work day, so the factory was a very subdued place after the New Year Eve celebrations.

The Parker Ballpen Refill

In 1955 the Parker Ballpen refill, which had been many years in the design stages in Parker Janesville, finally became manufactured in Newhaven.

Initially the point was made from bronze on Newhaven Tornos lathes, the cartridge shell was subcontracted with I.M.I, the ratchet and ink were sourced from America.

Pearl Eager demonstrating her manual dexterity in picking a minute pellet with tweezers to feed onto a nib blank.

Tom Hill, a Canadian who married a local girl whom he met while stationed in Newhaven with the Canadian Army during the Second World War. A most likeable man, he finished up as a much respected Factory Superintendent.

Assembly was carried out on single stage hand machines and was very laborious.

However, it was a very necessary learning curve. Both production staff and engineers learnt a great deal in the early stages, which was to serve them well, as gradually the whole process became fully automated and everything, apart from the ball, was made in house.

The Ballpen Refill was the first really high volume product to be produced in Newhaven, and over the years output consistently increased year on year and quality improvements were introduced, which made the Ballpen Refill a world beater.

Engineering Changes

In order to meet the factory requirements for better quality tooling and machinery, the Toolroom skill base was gradually built up.

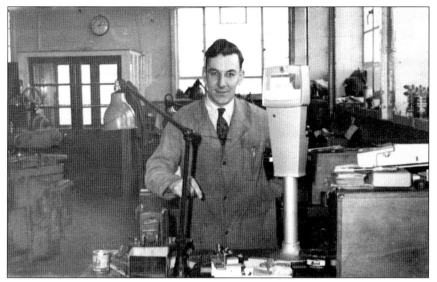

Malcolm Troak working on one of the six prototype parking meters which were made in the Newhaven toolroom.

The Toolroom had been re-housed in bays 1 and 2 of the new factory extension, which gave them the necessary space for new machines and bench areas.

Harold Smith (Smithy), who had been Chief Engineer from the early Valentine days, was due to retire in 1956. An outside replacement was recruited as Smithy's understudy in 1955. This was Len Porter, who was given the Toolroom as his first responsibility.

Unfortunately Smithy was to die a few months before his retirement, so Len Porter took over Engineering earlier than expected.

Smithy and Jack King were both practical jokers. Jack never tired of telling the story of how Smithy set him up one occasion.

The nib shop had just located to one of the bays in the new factory extension. Smithy and Jack King went to look at how the move had gone. Jack said: 'Look, how hard they are working because they know I am here. Smithy said: 'If you walked down the shop with that bottle between your legs, surely they would look up'. 'Definitely not' said Jack. He took the bottle, placed it between his legs and walked down the shop. He had got halfway when Smithy shouted out: "Kinger" at the

1957 and the Engineers Football Team to play the Office appear on East Side Recreation Ground. The team: Jim Parsons, Tim Harrison, Alan Lower, Ray Farley, Chris Creedon, Malcolm Troak, Alan Tapp, Bill Lees, Jock Lawson and Brian Troak.

top of his voice. The whole shop stopped working and looked at Jack with a bottle between his legs!

Management Changes

In 1952 Jack King was very deservedly given a Directorship on to the Main Board. From Newhaven's point of view this was an excellent move as it ensured Jack King would have direct access to the Main Board in London.

It did not end there, because in 1959 he was awarded an M.B.E. for the amount of Export Business which had been generated out of the Newhaven factory. Shortly after this he was made Managing Director of the Newhaven and Dover factories, another very popular move as far as the workforce were concerned.

When the accounting function was moved from Dover to Newhaven in 1953, Dickie Mansbridge relocated to Newhaven as well as a relatively unknown man, S.A. Dovey, who would not remain unknown for too long!

Another change came in 1957 when Arthur Marsden, who had worked in Dover and then in the London office, re-located to Newhaven as General Production Manager - the betting was that he would at some time replace Jack King.

Outside Consultants

In 1958 it was announced that for the first time a firm of Management Consultants had been employed to review current bonus schemes, where they existed, and to propose schemes where they did not.

This was naturally greeted with a fair amount of trepidation by the workforce who anticipated redundancies and changes to their working practices.

In the event it all went very smoothly and gave wonderful opportunities for several of the shop floor personnel to be trained as Work Study Officers, among these being Bernard Vaughan, Frank Bulman, Robin Tookey, George Witherspoon and John Attree.

Non Parker Products

During the 1950s there were several attempts by Parker Pen to diversify into different products. The person given responsibility for overseeing this was John Lee, who was based in the London Office. Here are brief details of three of the projects:

Flaminaire Lighters: A small service department was set up in the factory in order to have the facility to fill Flaminaire cigarette lighters with a special form of gas. Customers sent their lighters into Parker Pen for "topping up" with the special fuel which was dispensed at extremely low temperature. The section was closed down in the early sixties.

Parking Meters: An interest had been purchased in the Canadian Red Ball Parking Meter Company, with the objective of manufacturing and supplying parking meters to local councils, etc.

Six were built from scratch in the Newhaven Toolrom and received the Council of Design approval. The project was not pursued, however, because the margins were considered too low and it was recognised that Venner had already cornered the market in the U.K.

Tobacco Pipes: Cyril Ireland and Mavis Manners were the two Newhaven people who were seconded to the Pipe Project. A clear description of what was involved in the manufacture of a good

This happy group of men are enjoying the first Parker Toolroom Christmas Dinner at the Old Ship Hotel in Brighton in 1957.

The mid 1950s and the day shift is finished. It really was a mad exodus with cycles at that time certainly outnumbering cars, and all struggling to reach the railway level crossing gates first.

pipe has been left by Cyril. This has been re-printed in full as it makes very interesting reading.

Byford Pipes: It was during the early 1950s that tobacco pipes began to be manufactured at the Newhaven factory under the name of Byford Pipes, and Cyril became chargehand of the new enterprise. As far as he and his team were concerned, pipe making was a completely new and untried technique and they soon ran into technical problems. One major difficulty was the blending of the mouthpiece with the stem of the bowl and connector.

'Blending' was the creation of a smooth, perfect match at the point where the stem and the mouthpiece of the pipe were joined together - the bowl and the stem, of course, cut from briar wood while the mouthpiece was moulded from vulcanite and the connector was aluminum.

Although they tried hard they never really perfected it and eventually an established pipe manufacturer called Marcel Jacquemin took the contract to make Byford Pipes in his factory at Barking, Essex.

The unique feature of the Byford Pipe was that it had a capillary attraction system inside the stem, which trapped the moisture and gave a drier and cooler smoke than normal pipes. It was agreed that Cyril would spend time with Jacquemin's factory to find out all he could about the techniques of pipe making. Eventually it was decided that the

Jacquemim factory would be transferred to an empty building which stood in the Parker grounds. So, the machinery was all transferred to Newhaven where the Byford Pipe continued to be made by newly trained Parker staff, together with the Jacmar Pipe, the brand name of the Marcel Jacquemin products.

Dirty work: The moulding of the mouthpieces was done largely by hand and the finished shape on a special lathe, after which a hole was bored right through. The bowls were made from hardwood found in briar roots imported from France. These were roughly shaped from the block and then finished by hand and lathe. After which they were either sand-blasted to give a rough finish or polished for a smooth surface.

"It was very dirty work" says Cyril, "because when the barrel and the bowl were being blended together, the grinding process caused a lot of choking dust to float around and this problem was never successfully overcome."

For some years pipe making was one of the normal activities at Newhaven in its own special little factory.

A wonderful view of the factory taken in 1959 from the top of one of the remaining gasholders. Bays 1-9 can be seen in the foreground and a 'gaggle' of the very oldest buildings remaining in the centre of the picture.

As time went on some sub-contracting work was taken and the pipe factory began making components for other brands of pipes. Eventually the business was sold to the Orlik Pipe Company and pipe making finished in Newhaven.

Another Short Story:

A new girl started work in Bill Venus's department. The belt on her machine broke after an hours work, so she was told by Bill to take it to the Engineers who would repair it. She was a long time coming back with the belt still broken, when questioned by Bill she said "they didn't know what I was talking about" - it transpired she thought she had to go to the Engineer pub next door to the factory!!

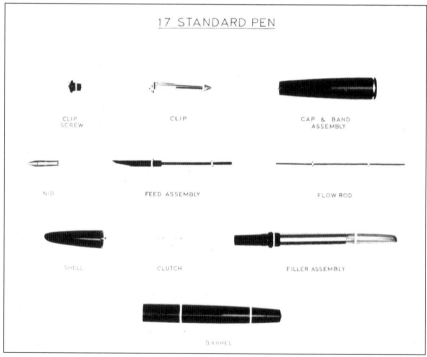

The '17' Range was designed and manufactured in Newhaven during the 1950s. It was initially produced by conventional machining methods but in 1961 was the first Newhaven product to have the cap and barrel produced by the injection moulding process.

CHAPTER 6

Parker Pen at Dover
1948 - 1968

Without doubt, if the decision to set up an extension or satellite factory in Dover had not been taken in 1948, the growth plans by Parker U.K. could have been badly thwarted. The 20 years duration of the Dover factory enabled Newhaven to carry out an extensive programme of building work and the establishment of a firm manufacturing base.

A short history of the Dover factory was written by Arthur Marsden in 1968 when he was Production Director at Newhaven.

It gives a very concise synopsis of the twenty years of Parker Pen in Dover and for that reason it is re-printed in this chapter.

The Dover Story

Just 20 years ago in August 1948, Ernest Woodcock and Jim Fitzgerald arrived in Dover from Newhaven to start up what was to become one of the largest ink manufacturing plants in the world. Parker had started a small ink production unit in Newhaven in January 1948 but with space at a premium, it had been decided to take over an existing factory in Dover.

Mr R. L. Mansbridge, the Financial Director, was responsible for starting and running the initial factory and was later succeeded by Mr G. Dowdeswell, who was Factory Manager there from 1949 to 1958, and then by Mr A.J. Reeves, the present Manager.

Started as an overflow factory for ink production, it shortly afterwards took over responsibility for all servicing and repair work. The servicing department was, at that time, operating in crowded and cramped conditions in Grosvenor Gardens and it seemed a logical move to transfer this, together with Messrs Novis and Diton and Miss Peaty and others, to the more spacious areas in Dover. With the vast increase in Parker business in the U.K. after the war, it was necessary to recruit and

This was the Parker Pen factory at Dover when it opened in 1948. The picture was taken from the top of the cliff overlooking the factory.

train a complete new servicing staff. At that time about 12 mechanics were taken on and trained, of whom a considerable number are still working in Dover.

Shortly afterwards, once again due to the tremendous demand for Parker products both home and overseas, the inspection, assembly and despatching functions were transferred from Newhaven to Dover. Messrs Bailey, Green and Franklin, all Newhaven staff, came over and had the job of recruiting staff and getting their departments to run at maximum efficiency. Coincident with this the Accounts Department and also the Export Shipping Department were transferred to Dover.

At its peak period, around the 1950s, the Dover factory employed over 300 people - even so, it was just not big enough to handle the workload and as a result of this, and the fact that legislation now permitted an extension to be built in Newhaven, most of the work in Dover, with the exception of the ink making and service departments, was transferred back to Newhaven. Later, in 1955, the accountancy and financial divisions were also moved over to the Sussex factory.

WHERE ONCE THE QUINK WAS MADE

The same view but a completely different building which replaced the Parker Pen factory. The new building was built initially to accommodate the newly launched hovercraft service to France in 1969.

In 1963 it was decided to try to utilise the remaining space to manufacture gift boxes, which had previously been bought from outside suppliers, and from this date, starting from scratch, the Box Department grew in strength to some 60 or 70 staff turning out one and a half million gift boxes a year.

All seemed set for this to continue until 1966, when Parker received notice from the Dover Harbour Board that the premises were required for harbour extension purposes.

This was necessary due to the expanding port traffic and the advent of the hovercraft era, all of which called for more space for the Dover Harbour Board in an already congested area. In 1966 all the staff in

Marksmen (and woman) of the Dover Parker Rifle Club who formed the 1951-2 team.

Dover were told of this and, regretfully, that the factory would have to close in July 1968.

Unsuccessful efforts were made to find suitable premises in the Dover area and, after much discussion, thought and heart-searching, it was decided to enlarge the factory at Newhaven to take over the Dover factory work.

All staff were given the opportunity to transfer to the Newhaven plant and those who could not do so, were being compensated and assisted in finding alternative employment

Jack King, who had developed a very firm relationship with the managers and staff in Dover, wrote the following message in the Pen and Ink Magazine of July 1968:

"It is a sad thing when a happy association with people you have known and worked with for 20 years is brought to an end by force of circumstance.

That a strong spirit of loyalty has existed in Dover has been amply demonstrated by the willing co-operation the staff have always given in their work, and by the consistent successes they have achieved in their social and sporting activities.

To the Dover staff, who have served the company so well through good times and difficult ones and who have not once failed to deliver to their promise, I would like to express my personal thanks, together with the sincere appreciation of all the Directors.

I shall always have very happy memories of our Parker people in Dover and I should like to wish each one every success in the future."

Transfers to Newhaven

The following members of Dover staff transferred to Newhaven in what was described as "fairly painless". There were certainly no real problems with integration, either within the Newhaven factory or in the local area.

Indeed, many of the staff transferred became first class line managers offering many skills to the Newhaven operation. Offspring of some of the transferred staff remain in the local area to this day, serving the community with the same degree of allegiance as their parents. Transferees from Dover to Newhaven:

Messrs J. Fitzgerald, H. Attree, W. Call, L. Hogben, C. Carr, Mrs M. McAdie and her daughter Miss B. McAdie, Messrs H. Diton, E. Tofts, B. Denmark, E. Robus, W. Hogben, J. Page.

Dover vs Newhaven

What is not generally known is that the U.K. Board of Directors had many long discussions in 1949 as to whether or not a decision should be made

Dover had tremendous traditions for social activities. On this occasion it was the Annual Christmas Dance at the Dover Stage in 1963.

with regard to the transfer of the total Newhaven factory to the new Dover factory.

Fortunately for Newhaven this was not carried forward and, in light of the lease expiry on the Dover factory in 1968, fortunate for all concerned.

Dover Stories

A Robbery: In 1951 a gang of thieves somehow climbed over the cliffs and got onto the roof of the Parker factory. Breaking in they managed to locate some £20,000 worth of gold nibs, which they stole and then re-climbed the steep cliff face. Nothing was ever recovered.

The Blue Seagulls: Shortly after the Quink plant was set up in Dover, the local press reported a strange phenomenon.

Apparently the seagulls around the Eastern Docks were sporting "Blue Bottoms" !! It was eventually discovered that blue dye used in the ink making process was escaping onto the roof where the seagulls used to settle.

A new extractor solved the problem.

The retirement of Jack Whittaker after working as a Delivery Driver for fourteen years. Jack is in the centre row.

CHAPTER 7
The 1960s

The sixties, just like the fifties, were the years of exceptional change and growth at Newhaven.

Changes, which were not only in key personnel but also in sustained technical advancement and joint consultation practices.

The growth came in the form of significant increased production output to meet ever growing sales requirements, headcount increases and an accelerated building programme.

1960 certainly started with a bang in Parker Pen Newhaven, with three firsts.

In January the first two storey extension of the factory was completed on time by local builders, Oxley & Bennett. It was described at the time as "one of the most modern factory buildings in south-east England".

The other first was the lunch time programme of "Workers Play Time" which was broadcast by the B.B.C. from the top floor of the new extension. It was the only area large enough to take all of the Newhaven staff.

The stars of the show were singers Dennis Lotis (who was to become famous), Peter Cavanagh, Betty Smith, the saxophone virtuoso, and the accompanying group of Bert Weedon, James Moody and Tim Bell.

The new assembly area was absolutely packed to capacity and it would appear that everyone had a marvellous time.

Finally the first issue of the first House Journal of the Parker Pen Company Ltd, England was launched in April 1960. It was entitled "Pen and Ink" and was produced until 1988 when the title changed to "Link". An ever popular read, it was completely "non political" and kept people updated on what was happening in the London Office, Dover and Newhaven, plus personal stories, memories, wedding photographs, etc.

The Longley Era

Early in 1962 Mr J.A. Longley joined Newhaven as Factory Manager in what was to be a roller coaster period in the Newhaven factory.

He had come with a good pedigree, a jet fighter pilot, and from his last job as Works Manager of the Mazda Valves Component factory.

A very tall, pipe smoking Yorkshire man, he attempted to put his mark on the manufacturing side from day one. He would call all the Foremen together for long and rather painful meetings and tell them exactly what he expected of them and their staff.

Jim Longley who was recruited for the position of Factory Manager at Newhaven. He joined early in 1962 with a good track record but somehow his management style failed to work in Newhaven and he resigned in November 1963.

His pet saying was "you will all go home tired but happy". One of his main projects was in his words "to weed out as quickly as possible all the dead wood in the factory".

This resulted in a great deal of fear on the shop floor, particularly when without too much warning forty people were sacked, with a warning that more would follow.

One slightly humorous story of this period concerned Wally Dunk, who was Nib Shop Foreman.

Mr Longley had an obsession about nib smoothness and was constantly on Wally's back to improve the writing smoothness of pen nibs.

On one occasion at the morning foreman's meeting in Mr Longley's office, Mr Longley said to Wally: "That batch of nibs you sent up last night was still too spiky, they were just like needles."

Of course Wally disagreed and asked to have a look for himself. Mr Longley went into his desk drawer and pulled out a brown envelope and slid it across his desk to Wally.

Wally looked inside and said: "Yes, I agree, they are much too sharp, but of course they would be, they are drawing pins." Mr Longley had pulled

In January 1963 the factory was once again badly flooded. This picture shows the area around the gatehouse in Railway Road. These floods actually acted as a "wakeup" call for the local authorities who implemented a drainage system which prevented any more flooding of the East Side area.

the wrong envelope from his desk drawer!

Another one of Mr Longley's obsessions was problems with the insert on the 61 shell. The 61 pen had just been launched in the U.K. with many of the components made in Newhaven, this included the 61 shell.

For some reason and quite randomly the gold insert, which was heat sunk into the plastic shell, would 'pop out'.

Mr Longley decided he could solve the problem and set up a course of action to eliminate the problem. Sample shells had to be delivered to his office at the end of each shift for testing.

On one occasion the night watchman on his rounds reported: "It was ten o'clock at night and the light was still on in Mr Longley's office. I looked in and observed him throwing plastic parts at the wall." Apparently this was a test he had thought up to check the adhesion of the insert to the shell!

Under Mr Longley's very demanding style of management things went from bad to worse, so much so that attempts were made by some of the operators to "get the Union in". In fact, many of the male operators did

No, not the ice age but February 1963 when the sea froze at Newhaven. It was so cold in the factory that the solid fuel boilers could not cope and extra heating units had to be hired.

take out a Union Card.

In the event Mr Longley did not last very long and he resigned in November 1963.

Stan Dovey - Factory Manager

Almost immediately Stan Dovey was promoted to replace him as Factory Manager, a job he set about with real enthusiasm.

In his previous job, Stan Dovey had been responsible to Mr Longley for Production Control, Purchasing and Work Study, so he would already have had his finger on the pulse of the manufacturing operations.

One of Stan Dovey's first actions was to set up a meaningful Factory Joint Consultative Committee, F.J.C.C. This was the platform for many far reaching operational changes made in Newhaven and was to put Parker in the forefront of good industrial practices.

Some of the more significant changes thrashed out at the F.J.C.C. were:

- Elimination of Tea Breaks with personnel allowed to use the supplied Drink Vending machines whenever required.

- The practice of "Clocking In" eliminated.

- Protected Bonus Scheme. Each operator on a performance related bonus scheme would be guaranteed their agreed level of bonus. This then gave a fixed weekly wage against a fluctuating wage under the old scheme.

- Reduction of the one-hour lunch break to half an hour. This resulted in an industry breaking week of 37.5 hours per week with Friday afternoons off.

Stan Dovey also set up Senior Management and Technicians evening meetings where common issues were all discussed and usually resolved.

The Sixties was certainly a period of accelerating change for the whole of the Newhaven site and it was fortuitous that Stan Dovey was at the helm to direct Engineering and Manufacturing.

One of his favourite sayings during this period was "We will accelerate the rate of change of the rate of change."

Production Engineering

A young Jim Hancock, who joined Parker Pen in December 1963 as the first Production Engineering Manager. A genial Cornishman with a flair for product design and manufacturing engineering, he soon built up a "World Class" team of engineers and designers.

In December 1962 Jim Hancock joined Parker Newhaven as its first Production Engineering Manager. It had been recognised for some time that Production Engineering was a key requirement if Parker were to advance technically.

In the event, Jim had an unusual introduction to Parker. He had been interviewed and offered the post by J. Longley. However, by the time Jim started, Longley had resigned and Jim's new boss was Stan Dovey!

Jim soon built up a very strong Engineering team, people of the calibre of Frank Wells, Bert Dyble, Harry Grint, Bob Barber, Don Allaway, to name but a few. Many of the Engineering changes resulted in the elimination of operator controlled jobs to machine controlled, particularly in the component producing areas.

Another area of great advancement was in injection moulding, specifically with regard to producing completely finished components straight off the machines.

Jim himself was instrumental in introducing the first moulded Pen Collector. This was the '45' Collector, where Jim had "stuck his neck on the block" and said it could be done. He was right, and the moulding of the Collector set the standard for many of the future moulding operations.

Another production Engineering success in the Sixties was the introduction of the stainless steel Ballpen Point on Swiss Albé machines. Also the mechanisation of the Ballpen Refill and T. Ball Jotter lines.

1960 and the start of the injection moulding age at Newhaven. This Peco Moulding Machine was purchased to specifically mould caps and barrels, Bernard Kingswood supervises the unloading.

Man at Work . . .

And the Peco at work moulding Lady Pen caps four at a time. The man at work is Bert Perryman who until his retirement continued to work in the moulding shop.

Without doubt, the Production Engineering Department was one of the cornerstones of Newhaven's future success stories, in both Engineering terms and new product introduction.

Car Parking becomes an Issue

One very noticeable change, which took place during the Sixties, was the gradual increase in those coming to work in a car.

Photographs of the early fifties show parking for no more than twelve cars, but sufficient room for around one hundred bicycles. Where to park your bike for a speedy departure was the order of the day!

Phil Brown, who was a well respected charge-hand, remembers his cycling days well:

Nearly everyone cycled to work and Phil vividly recalls the build up of traffic waiting at the level crossing gates for a train to pass. Those active enough to make sure of a place at the front cycled quickly clear, but those caught in the bunch risked coming a cropper on the railway line, which then ran across the bridge to the Western dock.

A larger car park on very rough ground was opened up on part of the old Gas Works site, to cater for the increased number of cars.

At one end there was a large gas holder still in place, which was retained as a reservoir for the local area. On one occasion without informing anybody at Parkers, the painters arrived to paint the Gasholder. They were using six inch brushes to "slap on" the Red Lead Primer when the wind suddenly changed direction and increased in strength.

A happy group of workers who have assembled in the newly built upstairs Assembly Department to watch the lunchtime show of the BBCs "Workers Playtime".

Betty Smith the Saxophone Virtuoso plays her part accompanied by Bert Weedon, James Moody and Tim Bell. The show was a huge success and was broadcast around the whole of the UK.

Work commences on the second half of the two storey building. In this photograph the gatehouse is being dismantled and the main entrance is to be re-sited on the north side of the factory. Railway Road appears incredibly quiet.

Suddenly, the cars in the Parker car park below were speckled with red lead paint.

There was absolute pandemonium when people dashed around trying to move their cars and attack the wet paint with white spirit!

Recruitment Issues

With the rapid increase in sales and the closure of the Dover Factory, recruitment of labour became a major issue for Newhaven. Having to recruit personnel to man a Quink Line, Despatch and Service Departments was no mean task for the personnel department, particularly Bernard Vaughan, whose main responsibility was factory labour recruitment.

There was also a major task in training female staff for the Repair Department within Service. In Dover, repairs had been carried out by males, but it was agreed that with the new products on line it was possible for females to carry out this work. A role they carried out superbly.

A Newhaven "School Shift" was even started for 16 year olds, who would come to the factory on a Saturday morning to assist with the packaging operation.

The new entrance for Parker Pen factory and offices. Notice the new car park on the left and the "builders shed" acting as a temporary gatehouse.

Eventually it was decided during 1960 that coaches would have to be used by Parker to bring and return workers recruited from the more outlying areas. This certainly helped to overcome what might have been a serious situation.

To accommodate all the extra staff, work started at the end of 1960 with an additional two storey block, adjoining the block already built facing Railway Road, and a much larger Canteen and Kitchen block. This unfortunately meant the end of the Tennis Court!

At the same time Newhaven's first IBM Computer was installed, this being the responsibility of Sid Purbrick. The computer was an IBM 360/20 and was used mainly to provide financial and sales information. It was realised even at this stage in 1966 that upgrades in terms of larger computers would soon be required to meet Manufacturing Management's needs.

Christmas at Parker's

In the days before "drink driving" and stringent Health and Safety regulations, Christmas could be quite a riotous time at Parker Pen.

Christmas parties would start two or three weeks before the actual factory closure with the Departmental Parties, two of the largest being the Assembly Department and the Plastics Shop. These would be on separate weeks and usually upstairs in the Newhaven Conservative Club.

The following days after these parties would be full of "who did what", etc. etc.

Most of the other departments would also hold their own separate dinners / parties.

The Engineers (Toolroom and Maintenance) held two very memorable Dinners at the old Ship Hotel, Brighton which even to this day are still talked about!

A few days before Parker's closed for Christmas, the Canteen staff would put on a wonderful Christmas Dinner in the Canteen. Real turkey and their own make of Christmas pudding was the order of the day.

The Feed and Collector Section before it was replaced with the introduction of injection moulded components. Tom Winton the "Feed Supremo" sits front centre and is setting up on a small lathe.

A nice inside picture of the autos and plastics section found within the "New Shop". Los Cowley is the man in the white coat. It all looks very quiet, but it never was and was an extremely noisy area in which to work.

Railway Road. The old entrance has already disappeared and as can be seen work is well under way on the two storey extension.

Probably the most riotous time for the shop floor, but certainly not for the foremen and charge-hands, was the final working day before Christmas. Particularly in the early sixties when there was no half day on the final day and considerable numbers would be out to the local pubs for a lunch time drink. These were certainly memorable days for all concerned!

There are two incidents which reflect these times.

1. Jim Parsons from the Toolroom was reported calling into the Gatehouse early on the morning after the Christmas shutdown. He was looking for his false teeth! Apparently, he had had a drink, felt sick, so he took his dentures out, put them on the wash basin, and then gone home without them! Fortunately, he found them where he had left them.

2. The Night Watchmen on his rounds after the factory had closed, heard strange noises coming from the Carpenter's Workshop. When he got the key and opened the door, he found a young man lying out on the bench. Apparently, this lad (who still lives locally) had drunk too much, felt bad and decided to have a rest in the Carpenter's Shop. As it was one o'clock in the morning, he obviously had to walk home!

From the Pen & Ink

August 1966. They work hard at Newhaven - even during the holidays! During the month of July an exceptional amount of overtime has been worked at the Newhaven Factory due to the unprecedented demand for Parker products. The total overtime amounted to an impressive 2,000 hours per week.

During each of the first two weeks of August, when the factory was 'officially closed', 50 people voluntarily gave up their holiday to come to work! This confirms what we have always thought and often said - our own Parker people and the products we make have the same thing in common - QUALITY!

November 1967 Was this a premonition? You May Soon Cook By Microwaves. In the not too distant future it is possible that microwave cookers will be as common in British kitchens as gas and electric ones are today. Using a completely new principle for home cookery, which

This is a view of the new assembly department upstairs in the two storey extension. Bill Hogben is on the right with his head down and the white coat. Assembly was still a very labour intensive hand operation at this time, and automated assembly was still a few years away.

This is the Badalex Assembly Machine. It was the first piece of automatic assembly equipment used in the Assembly Department. It was designed to assemble a complete T Ball Jotter cap.

works on radio waves, the microwave cookers promise to save the housewife about 75 per cent of her time in the kitchen and they'll be cheap to operate too - using only about the same amount of current as an electric kettle.

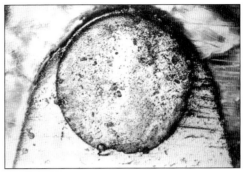

No, not the surface of the moon, but a section cut through a ballpen refill ball! It highlights all the little 'craters' which helped the ball to 'grip' the paper when writing.

IT WAS A PROUD DAY FOR THE TUTT FAMILY—

Richard Tutt is proudly carrying his indenture papers having completed his Toolmaking Apprenticeship with Parker. His father, Iden and mother, Kathy are on his left and both also worked at Parker Pen. Cyril Ludlum the Toolroom Foreman is on the right.

Cyril Green, a much respected senior foreman. He was taught to assemble the first '51' Pens in Newhaven, spent several years in the Dover plant before transferring back to his home town of Newhaven. Before retirement he was responsible for all the Newhaven assembly operations.

This old building was known as "The Pipe Shop" because it was here that the Byford Pipe was made. It was demolished during the 1960s to make way for a new gatehouse and to increase the number of car parking spaces.

George Witherspoon is shown holding a training session for a large number of new starters. Due to the large number of starters during the 1960s a quite intense induction programme was introduced. On the right hand wall is the master clock which controlled starting and finishing bells.

They all wave the productivity flag

This picture taken outside the factory in 1962 shows a group of workers who had all contributed 'workable ideas' during National Productivity Year.

No. Parkers who purchased the East Side Mission Hall in Baker Street hadn't suddenly gone all religious! The hall became redundant so it was purchased by Parker Pen who demolished it and formed a southern access route to the factory.

1968 and the Service Department which transferred to Newhaven when Dover closed is shown up and running in its new location.

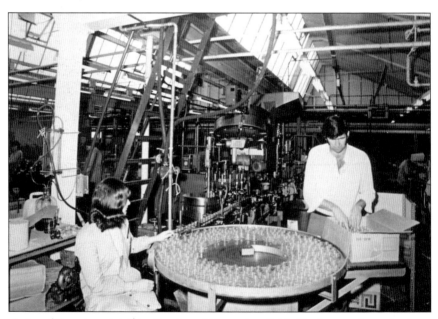

A view of the automatic ink bottling line which was installed in Newhaven prior to the closure of the Dover factory.

This picture speaks for itself. The Royal Warrant was awarded to the Parker Pen Co in 1962.

This delightful photograph of Bob Strudwick was taken by Monty Lane. Bob, a wonderful character used to keep the factory spick and span for many years.

Monty Lane who was an avid photographer and supplied many photographs for 'Pen and Ink' is 'caught' by another photographer!

The first staff coaches line up outside the factory in Railway Road. They were used to collect and return workers to the outlying areas where transport could be a problem, and to help solve a labour shortage.

This picture shows one of the first drinks vending machines introduced into the factory when the tea breaks were eliminated. The drinks dispensed were described as being "variable"!

The '45' clip progression tool is shown here in its full glory. Instead of around 15 separate operations this tool produced one 45 clip per stroke, a very important saving in both time and labour.

This photograph shows the injection moulded 45 collector. Technically this was a major achievement and set the path for Newhaven's rapid advance in the field of injection moulding.

1968 and the new Canteen and Kitchen blocks are under construction on the site of the old Tennis Courts. The one remaining Gasholder, soon to be demolished still looms gloomily over the whole Factory site.

A very good view of the Newhaven Toolroom in 1968 which shows its position relative to Bays 1 and 2. Every available space appears to have been utilised particularly in the Grinding Section!!

CHAPTER 8
The 1970s

During the 1970's Newhaven was faced with a great many difficulties. These ranged from that ugly word "inflation", extended power-cuts and power sharing, and significant shortfalls in labour.

There were also Newhaven produced new products to manufacture and introduce with very short lead times, and also the implementation of a new computer which was to embrace all of the Newhaven factory.

Mr A. F. Marsden who was Managing Director when his untimely death was announced on Saturday 12th May 1979. A quiet, unassuming man, who was much respected by his colleagues who had worked under his successful management since he had been promoted to lead the company in 1972.

In spite of all these problems it was reported in 1979 that, "year after year the figures of Production and Sales climb to new higher levels, and each year it appears that the absolute limit has been achieved. However such is the expertise, enthusiasm and dedication of everyone concerned that seemingly impossible heights have once again been reached."

Fortunately, many of the actions already implemented, such as new Factory and Office Building, a larger Canteen, new Boiler House, improved car parking helped some of the problems, but obviously not all of them.

Labour Shortages

In the Newhaven and Lewes area during the 1960s/70s there had been a considerable number of factories and warehouses built, all of which obviously required staffing.

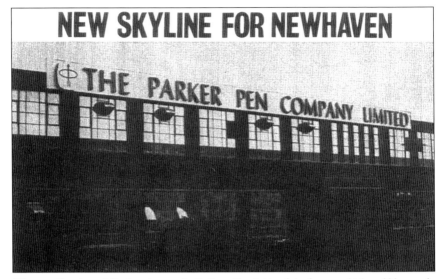

The new illuminated Parker sign on the Railway Road side of the factory which could be seen by both rail and road passengers by day and night.

There was therefore considerable demands for labour in the local area particularly for female staff, and for the first time Parker Pen began to feel the pinch.

Not that Parker lost many staff to these new ventures, it was just that with production requirements increasing almost weekly significantly more staff were required by Parker Pen.

It was a time for innovative thinking! As well as many varied and eyecatching advertisements in the local area, various schemes were implemented to attract labour.

One particular scheme, which was very successful, was an Introduction Bonus Scheme. Any employee introducing a new employee to the Company would receive a £5 bonus, plus a further £20 when the new member had completed eight weeks employment. In 1973 this was considered a very good reward, and staff responded positively. Evening shifts were made available to typists, clerks, computer operators, etc. who would all take their places beside the regular factory personnel working late into the night in order to keep production flowing and sales orders met. Another very popular scheme introduced in the Autumn of 1974 was the 'Parker Christmas Cracker Scheme'

HUNDREDS OF PRIZES

HERE'S YOUR PARKER PEN CHRISTMAS CRACKER ALBUM full of luxurious and practical things for yourself, your family, your home, hobbies and garden. It also gives you a wonderful opportunity of solving your Christmas present problem.

IT IS OUR WAY OF SAYING 'THANK YOU' for the overtime effort necessary over the next 13 weeks so that home and export customers get their orders in time for Christmas.

YOU EARN PRIZE POINTS IN ADDITION TO YOUR OVERTIME PAY for every hours overtime worked, provided you do 7 or more hours in any calendar week.

WE PAY YOUR TAX, so your prizes on this scheme are tax free.

HERE'S HOW YOU WIN YOUR PRIZE

WORK 7 HOURS OR MORE OVERTIME IN any week during September,

October or November.

100 PRIZE POINTS for every hour's overtime you work is credited to you.

It obviously had the desired effect! The factory overtime worked in the twenty six weeks prior to the Cracker scheme being implemented was an average of 1,700 hours per week and during the duration of the scheme an average of 3,400 hours per week.

Another scheme was an attempt to recruit suitable staff from the Manchester area. This was not a success and resulted in just three girls coming to Newhaven to work.

One bone of contention during this period of excessive overtime requirements came from many of the female operators. They told management that they would willingly work on Sundays, but unfortunately at that time, the old Factories Act would not allow it. In fact, the Act was particularly restrictive in terms of working hours for both young persons and older females.

At one time in the late seventies a record number of over 1,000 people were employed in Newhaven. It was quickly realised by the Senior Management team that this could not continue and plans were put in place to automate many of the operations carried out by hand. Any new product had to be designed with this in mind, something which Newhaven designers and engineers became very good at, particularly with regard to automatic assembly.

The Winter of Discontent

Newhaven like every other business in the country was affected by power cuts and restrictions in the winter of 1971/72, which had been brought on by the Miners' strikes.

Parker's electrical consumption at Newhaven was restricted from Midnight to Midnight on Tuesdays, Fridays, Saturdays and Sundays leaving only three days for full production.

Not only were machines out of action on the restricted days but, of course, there was no heat or lighting for those people who did work because their jobs did not require power. To make the most of daylight therefore some staff started earlier than normal and cut lunch breaks down to half an hour.

Operators who normally worked shifts extended their hours so that their machines - moulders, automatics, and point making machines - were in operation from midnight to midnight on the power days. Many other operators worked on until after 9 p.m. on the power days. Maintenance staff covered the full week to deal with the technical problems that inevitably arose. Laboratory and office staff coped with difficult lighting conditions and Data Preparation girls worked unusual hours, with one shift from midnight to 8 a.m., on the power days.

Staff reactions to these adverse circumstances were so fantastic that orders suffered only slight delays and output was hardly affected. No one suffered financially through short hours, and the majority, by re-arrangement, completed their normal working week.

The '25' Range

The idea of the '25' Range was first mooted by the UK Sales Force early in the 1970s.

They wanted a new product range which would appeal to the eighteen to thirty year old group, a section of some ten million people who had never been specifically targeted by Parker.

It was felt that this group would be receptive to something modern in materials and styling but still with Parker quality. This was the very basic remit given to the Newhaven Product Design and Engineering teams.

After much discussion it was agreed that use should be made of a recognised outside designer with a proven track record in the design of modern consumer goods.

In the event the person selected was Kenneth Grange who had produced designs for a good range of modern products.

From Newhaven's Manufacturing and Engineering point of view their requirements were very simple - the least number of parts, designed for automatic assembly with simple finishing processes, and very minimum servicing/repair requirements.

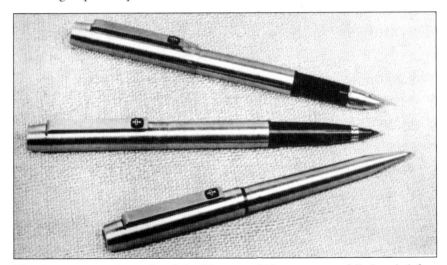

The three main writing modes of the 25 range which was so successfully launched from Newhaven in 1970.

An interesting advertisement for the new Fibre Tip Refill. This refill was designed and manufactured solely in Newhaven during 1970.

Kenneth Grange presented many designs, some were 'too modern' for Parker and some were even classed as outrageous. Eventually however a suitable 'All Stainless Steel' model range was agreed.

Detailed component design was completed in the Newhaven Design Office, which included a completely new one-piece feed collector system, which met all the latest requirements for air travel.

Even the nib was made from special Stainless Steel and used for the first time a completely spherical ball which could be automatically fed to the nib for welding.

The Stainless Steel Caps and Barrels also taxed the Engineers' skills to the limits as they were Deep Drawn, a process which had only recently been established in Newhaven.

One major departure from Parker Product design concepts was a 'flat clip' dispensing with the traditional feathered versions.

From a Newhaven Manufacturing and Engineering perspective the 25 product range was a great success. All the very tight schedules and quality aspects were achieved on time and the launch dates were achieved.

When the 25 Range was introduced at the UK Sales Conference in June 1975, it was described in the following manner:

"The styling of the new 25 models is a somewhat startling departure from previous Parker designs, gone is the subtle tapering - instead there are straight sided profiles. The brushed Stainless Steel is enlivened with blue plastic symbol motifs on the simple straight clips. There are blue plastic trims on bands and caps.

Production Engineer, Owen Jones sets one of the newly installed Deep Draw Presses at Newhaven in 1976. This was the first of many of these presses to be installed at Newhaven. They produced stainless caps and barrels plus many other internal and external metal components.

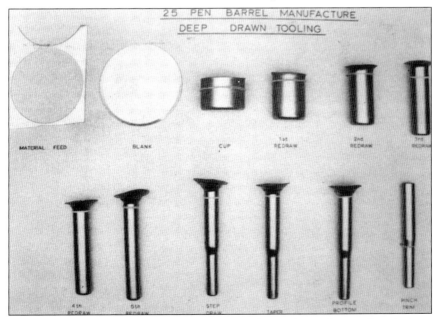

A layout showing the eleven stages in the production of a stainless steel 25 pen barrel using a deep draw press.

VDUs (visual display units) were gradually introduced into all areas of Newhaven. In this picture we can see Miss Terry Powell of the Export Department under Training with Derek Williams, Systems Manager.

During 1976 the Marketing Department moved from Grosvenor Gardens, London to Newhaven. The ladies in the picture are just some of those who formed part of the Marketing Department in Newhaven.

The Fountain Pen has a stainless steel nib and a completely new and modern ink feed system.

The Pen will retail at £4, the Ballpen at £3, and the Fibretip at £2.50."

There was obviously some reservations from the Sales Force regarding the latest product offering. This was mainly down to the 'Modernistic' design which was quite different to anything previously produced in Newhaven.

However with very powerful advertising and the dedication of the UK Sales Force the 25 Range sold well, particularly as a school pen - it was virtually indestructible!

Later on in 1978 when the 25 Black Matte range was introduced, sales increased considerably, particularly within the original target market of eighteen to thirty year olds.

Other Newhaven designed products, which were introduced during the 1970s, were the Lady Ballpens in white and yellow rolled gold, and subsequently in a lacque finish.

The '105' Range featured a spring loaded clip and a completely new 'Bark Finish' in Rolled Gold. This method of finishing caps and barrels was developed 'inhouse' by a Parker engineer Shaun Clay. It enabled a deep indentation to be formed even on a thin layer of rolled gold.

The 105 Range was introduced to meet a recognised gap in the UK Market in the higher price range. Unfortunately, the product offering never really sold through, and when the price of gold suddenly escalated it was phased out in 1983.

Changes at Newhaven

In June 1976 the Marketing department transferred from their offices in Grovesnor Gardens in London to a new base in Newhaven. This was the first in a series of moves before Grovesnor Gardens was eventually shut down in 1982.

The Marketing Staff came under the control of Jacques Margry, Marketing Director, who stated that there were significant benefits in being much closer to the product development and manufacturing unit.

NEW APPRENTICES TO PARKER

1970 and a new intake of Toolroom Apprentices. The three Apprentices with their parents are Bryndon Guy, Kieran Packham and Peter Easton.

October 1977 and Henry Ditton, fourth from the right, retires from Parker Pen having worked with the company for a record 49 years. He had previously worked in Bush House, then Dover and transferred to Newhaven when Dover closed.

One unforeseen change came about when Arthur Marsden who had been the Managing Director since 1972 on the retirement of Jack King, passed away suddenly on 12 May 1979.

One of his last actions at Newhaven was to approve the introduction of P.P.P. which stood for the Parker Positive Progress campaign.

Following the death of Arthur Marsden, Stan Dovey was appointed Chief Executive of the UK Company.

His personal message was:

"To accept the responsibility for a company the size of Parker Pen, U.K. is a challenge. But to accept Parker Pen with its past record performances and excellent results would normally be a daunting task.

Fortunately Arthur Marsden, our late Managing Director, had organised the Parker Positive Progress Campaign just before his untimely death and this is having considerable beneficial effects. As in the past special campaigns it is obvious already that your special efforts will lead to dramatic improvements in Company performance.

Particularly encouraging has been the exceptional number of sensible suggestions put forward, many of which have already been implemented with resultant cost savings. Larger projects have been identified and are being pursued with enthusiasm.

I have always been pleased and very impressed with the achievements when special efforts have been called for and I am sure that staff in all divisions will make the Parker Positive Progress Campaign a resounding success".

One major organisational change in August 1977, which indirectly affected Newhaven, was the appointment of Willi Seiberger to the position of North American Area Manager.

In this position he had the full responsibility for the marketing of writing instruments in the United States and Canada.

Willi Seiberger had been the General Manager of Parker Pen Germany for fourteen years and had built Parker into a major force in the German writing instrument business.

The appointment was taken as a reflection of the increasingly poor level

The Assembly and Service Department meet the third Guide Dog for the Blind which they had "purchased" from collections and raffles in the departments. In this case the monies had been collected by Miss Emons and Mrs Pearse.

of sales in the American Domestic markets. It was also an indication of some of the problems the Parker Pen Company would have to face up to in the 1980's.

Jottings from the Seventies

'A Very Lucky Girl' Maureen Beal went through some extremely worrying days when she lost her diamond engagement ring. When Maureen, who worked in Despatch Department, missed the ring she realised that it must have been pulled off her finger into one of the cartons she had been packing for despatch to dealers. Unfortunately, by that time the cartons had already left the factory on the way to various parts of the country. Maureen asked the Order Department to help and phone calls were made to the likely dealers requesting them to search their parcels carefully for the ring.

Then came the news from Messrs. Binns Ltd in Newcastle-on-Tyne that the ring had been found - among the packing paper in their carton. A couple of days later Maureen was elated to receive her precious ring safely back again.

'**New Skyline for Newhaven**' The prestige of Parker at Newhaven should now be even higher than before because of a new dominating illuminated sign on the front of the factory building which can be seen from miles around the area. This new addition to the Newhaven skyline replaces the old Parker sign which was in a very dated style of lettering. The new sign, in the standard Parker lettering called 'Optima', reflects the modern image associated with Parker products.

Anthony Trafford, Director of the Renal Unit at the Royal Sussex County Hospital chats to Pat Burnard in the Assembly Department. He was visiting the department to thank them all for the cheque presented to him to help run kidney machines at the hospital.

The Factory Management Team admiring the newly installed Bruderer Press. This press was designed to take progression tools which in turn would produce clips and other metal components significantly faster than conventional means.

These are some of the labour intensive presses which were replaced when the Bruderer press was up and running.

June 1977 - The Silver Jubilee, and the captions say it all. This is just one small group who enjoyed a free ice cream courtesy of the Parker Pen Co when the special ice cream van toured Newhaven street parties and the carnival on the 8th and 9th of June.

A Parker Quink Plant was set up in India during the 1960s by the UK Company. This interesting vehicle is being used to deliver Quink in Delhi.

Colleagues in Newhaven were shocked to hear of the death of Len Porter and George Witherspoon following a tragic car accident on Saturday 20th June 1970. They were on a weekend visit to Swaziland from neighbouring South Africa where Len was Chief Engineer in Parker's factory. Len had moved to South Africa in 1966 from the Newhaven factory where he had served many years as the engineering manager.

John Devereux who was for many years the Industrial Chaplain in the Newhaven factory. He helped many people with their problems and concerns, in a very kind, considerate and totally confidential manner.

March 1971 and "Tupps" Strudwick retires after 42 years service. She is seen in this photograph receiving her retirement gift from Dan Parker who happened to visit the factory. Jack King looks on beaming.

Photographed in June 1973 this happy group had all just completed 25 years service with Parker Pen.

Tony Gasson of Quality Control and Helen Burnett of the Ballpoint Department after their wedding on 3rd May 1975.

A beaming Grace Jameson presents a Parker Pen to Dame Flora Robson who had just toured the factory. This took place in December 1974 and the Christmas decorations can just be seen.

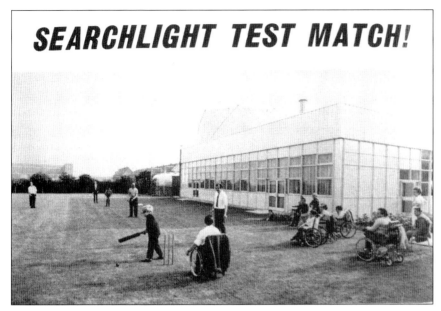

The Newhaven factory always had a happy relationship with the Searchlight Home and supported them in all sorts of ways. This picture shows the "special" cricket match after the annual BBQ in 1971.

The 1976 Lewes to Newhaven Annual Raft Race on the River Ouse. It would appear the Parker crew are heading for the opposite bank!

In 1977 Boots celebrated their centenary 1877 - 1977. To celebrate this event they ordered a record breaking 68,000 Custom Insignia Ballpens suitably engraved from Parker Pen. These were to be distributed to staff and special customers. The 1850 stagecoach was used to deliver the final batch to the Boots Head Office in Nottingham.

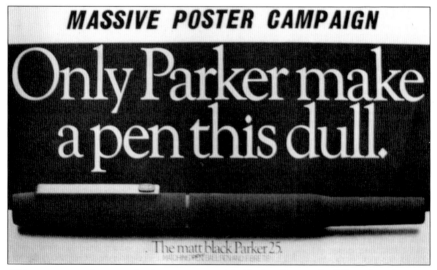

This poster campaign was the largest ever used by Parker Pen in the UK to launch a new product. It proved its worth with significantly early sales of the Matte Black 25.

CHAPTER 9
The 1980s

Whoever wrote the headline article in the January 1980 issue of the Pen and Ink must have had a Crystal ball.

The Headline in very bold print said.
"Parker prepares for a decade of change confidently into the 'eighties'"
How right they were!!

For the people in the Newhaven factory 1980 started very pleasantly when 1200 Parker people and guests sailed to Dieppe aboard the M.V. Senlac on April l9th.

The day trip was the Company's way of saying "thank you" to all the staff who had contributed so positively to the P.P.P. campaign.

Controlled by Paul Osbourne, Manufacturing Manager and assisted by Jim Fitzgerald, John Owen and Remi Pollard, the Parker Positive Progress Campaign was a huge success with savings yielding £200,000 per annum and cost reductions a further £150,000.

The M.V. Senlac was chartered for the whole day and was for Parker Staff and their friends and relatives only. Seaford Silver Band was on board and gave a splendid rendering of "A life on the Ocean Wave" as the Senlac left Newhaven bound for Dieppe.

Once in Dieppe there were coach trips to Rouen, Fecamp or the Dieppe Hypermarket for anybody who wanted to visit these places.

April 1980 and the first Parker group climb the gangway ready to board the M.V. Senlac on the day trip to Dieppe.

These three happy girls, Glynis Easton, Janice Cager and Denise Pateman are helping to ship a large order of Roller Balls.

Everybody apparently had a marvellous day and left the Senlac asking, 'well, when is the next trip'?

New Product Introductions

During the 1980s a whole range of new products designed and manufactured in the Newhaven factory were introduced to the marketplace.

These ranged from the RB 1 designed as a holder for the Roller Ball Refill, the Harlequin range which utilised Newhaven's excellent acid etching capability, the very prestigious Duofold Centennial Pen and finally the 88 Range.

The RB 1, which was perhaps the most functional product, quickly established itself as a brand leader in this particular segment of the marketplace.

It was the brainchild of Jacques Margry who quickly realised the sales potential of the Parker Roller Ball Refill as a profitable alternative to the well established ball pen refill.

Jack Finalay who sadly died on 5th June 1980. Over many years Jack made a contribution in developing and maintaining good working relationships throughout the Newhaven factory. He had the ability to communicate effectively with all levels to find common ground for agreement. Jack was dedicated to improving the quality of life for all, and in this respect his contribution to the company over many years was considerable. Jack had a tremendous personality characterised by his sense of humour, which enabled him to make light of his own physical disability.

November 1981 and the very last of the old Valentine buildings are being demolished for more modern 'clear span' workshops to be erected.

In order to maximise the full potential of the Parker Roller Ball refill he requested that a suitable holder be designed and manufactured as quickly as humanly possible.

Designed basically on the back of a 'cigarette packet' by a handful of Newhaven people, the RB1 was presented to marketing, agreed and approval given to manufacture the model.

The only really design constraint was the clip. Willi Seiberger had decreed that "all" clips should follow the design of the two-piece Arrow Clip. Newhaven had to initially abide by the ruling although a 'one piece' stainless steel clip was already waiting in the wings!

After a very very successful launch complaints started to arrive about both breakage and the degree of 'sharp edges' on the two piece clip. Agreement was soon reached that it would be in order to change over to the stainless steel 'one piece' clip. Newhaven had produced a world beater.

The other plus point about the RB 1 was the long parallel barrel and cap which were absolutely ideal for printing purposes. The Newhaven Industrial Marking section produced many stunning designs in multicolours and, in fact won, many prestigious awards for their work on these products.

Receptionist, Yvonne Preece seen here polishing the beautiful brass Parker Arrows which previously adorned the Grosvenor Gardens office in London.

Eventually the range was extended with a pen, pencil and ball pen and renamed Vector.

It has often been said that imitation is the sincerest form of flattery, so it was not long before many poor copies of the Vector Range were discovered. Fortunately none of the counterfeit products affected sales of the genuine Parker Vector and the range continues to sell well to this day.

Duofold Centennial

In 1987 the famous Parker Duofold was re-introduced as the Duofold Centennial Fountain Pen and Ballpen.

The phasing of the introduction was in anticipation of the 100th anniversary of Parker Pen.

Designed and manufactured in Newhaven it was an immediate success providing traditional Parker classic pen styling with state-of-the-art writing technology.

Many of the external parts were produced on computer numerically controlled (CNC) machinery which enabled very close tolerances and finishes to be maintained.

The nib was a masterpiece of traditional craftsmanship with no less than 21 individual operations from start to finish.

Sales worldwide were so successful that in order to keep up with demand the parent company in Janesville set up its own manufacturing facility.

Over time the range was expanded with the introduction of a slimmer International Fountain Pen, Rollerball and Pencil.

The Duofold Centennial range demonstrated very clearly that it was possible to re-create a sixty year old product by using modern materials and technology and compete with the best. It also put Newhaven Design, Engineering and Manufacturing firmly on the top of the ladder within the Parker Worldwide Group.

A Collector's Item

We know that the Premier Collection is of sufficient importance for it to become of interest to collectors in the future. We also know that this special Premier - bearing one of the first production numbers - will have a particular significance as a collector's item.

Please accept it with our best wishes and our thanks for joining us and helping us to make history in Monte Carlo.

✦ PARKER

PARKER PREMIER
MONTE CARLO
1983

PRINCIPAUTE
DE MONACO

A collector's card which was included with the premier range when launched in Monte Carlo in 1983.

The European Distribution Centre

In early 1983 Newhaven was inaugurated as the new Area Headquarters for the Parker European, African and Middle East operations.

At the same time it was announced that Newhaven would become the centre for distribution for the whole of the European area.

In order to cope with the future volumes of orders for distribution approval was given for the construction of a purpose built warehouse on a site to the East of the factory. The site in fact was always known as the Twelve acre field' and had been purchased on Jack Kings recommendation for a few hundred pounds in the 1940s - a far sighted investment.

When built the warehouse, or Brown Barn as it was affectionately called, covered 50,000 square feet (4,645 square metres) with just two spans. It was, when built, one of the largest warehouses of its type on the South Coast.

Under the direction of David Smith and ably assisted by John Owen the EDC soon became a centre of excellence for distribution within the Parker empire.

Changes at the Top

Between 1982 and 1985 there were many significant management

The European Distribution Centre which was built in Newhaven to meet an increasing demand for Parker products across Europe. It was affectionally nicknamed the 'Brown Barn' because of its colour.

changes made at the Writing Instrument Group headquarters in Janesville which had a direct impact on the Newhaven factory.

These changes were implemented primarily because Parker's sales and profits had suffered from a World Recession and, more specifically, the strength of the U.S. Dollar. It was also recognised that the very high cost structure, associated with Parker's style of operation in the USA, needed to change.

The slightly concerned look on the group looking up was because the Chief Executive, James Margry, was taking a ride in the newly installed high-lift shelf loader. He did eventually land safely!

In early 1982 Manville Smith, a relative newcomer to the American company, was promoted to the position of President of the Writing Instrument Group (WIG) and virtually at the same time Jim Peterson was recruited to head up the Parker Pen Company as Group President and CEO. Both of these new

Paul Osbourne who died aged 43 in June 1985. A Director of the company, Paul was certainly being groomed for a position of high responsibility with Parker Pen. An energetic and very forward looking manager who created many significant changes in his area of responsibility, he was very sadly missed.

Stan Dovey retired from Parker Pen in 1985. He was responsible for many of the fundamental changes in the Newhaven factory during the 1960s and 1970s, and many more particularly with the introduction of improved working practices and industrial relations.

appointments were based in the Parker Pen headquarters in Janesville.

One of Manville Smith's early plans was to enter the low margin mass market for disposable writing instruments. In order to do this agreement was reached to close the Arrow Park facility from May to Nov 1983 to enable work to commence to totally re-equip and remodel the American factory.

Newhaven were told that they would have to supply world demand during the projected six month renovation period.

The Newhaven factory certainly rose to the challenge and during the month of July for example produced well in excess of a million pens per week.

In spite of many changes, the extensive use of top level management consultants and huge capital investment programmes, results were not forthcoming. It was therefore no surprise to receive notification from the office of Jim Peterson that very stringent cuts would have to be made in all areas just to 'break even' in FY85.

At this period in time there were two main players in the Parker Pen Company. These being the Writing Instrument Group and Manpower Inc.

In March 1976 The Parker Pen Company had obtained a majority interest in Manpower Inc. an up and coming company which provided temporary help services to all types of business.

It was run very successfully as a completely separate entity to the Writing Instrument Group. Within a very short time Manpower Inc. grew very rapidly and became the predominant "division" within the Parker Pen Company, generating excellent margins and profits.

In 1985 the Senior Management of Parker Pen decided to withdraw from the writing instrument business by disposing of the whole of the Writing Instrument Division. The reason for the sale came from the consistent strength of the American Dollar over many years, creating difficulties for American Companies dealing in large export volumes. Parker, with 75% of its sales outside of the U.S.A., was exposed to any adverse currency fluctuation.

Fortunately the vast majority of personnel within the Newhaven factory were unaware of all that was going on across the Atlantic, they just carried on what they were best at - making and selling pens!

The Management Buy-out

Once the Directors based in Newhaven become aware of the imminent sale of the Writing Instrument Group, they discussed possible ways of effecting a Management Buy-out of the group.

Initially Jacques Margry, Bob Barnsley and Peter Mettyear set the wheels in motion, they had to first establish what constituted a management Buy-out. Gradually other Directors were brought into the discussions and the final team consisted of Jacques Margry, Bob Barnsley, Peter Kibble, Peter Mettyear, Barrie Robinson and Malcolm Troak.

The buy-out group's original plans were to make a bid for just the European Operation, but this was categorically turned down by Parker Pen.

There was to be no "cherry picking" it was the whole Writing Instrument Group or nothing!

1986 and this group of Directors were the driving force in the Management Buyout of Parker Pen. This brought the worldwide headquarters to Newhaven. Left to right: Messrs Mettyear, Margry, Kibble, Troak and sitting are Barnsley and Robinson.

A buy-out team was therefore put together which comprised members of the Parker Management team, certain Venture capital funds advised by Schroeder Ventures, which was headed by Jon Moulton, Chemical Equity Associates, Bankers Trust International Ltd., Electra Investment P.L.C. and PKR Associates representing various interests of the Parker Family.

After significant negotiation the business of the Parker Group was acquired in January 1986 and Parker Pen Limited, the new company established its headquarters in Newhaven.

This was an incredible episode in Newhaven's history which just over forty three years previously had been a very poor relation to the giant parent company in America.

1988 - The Parker Centennial Year

It was in 1888 that George Safford Parker, a 25 year old teacher from Janesville Wisconsin U.S.A., invented his first successful fountain pen and subsequently incorporated the Parker Pen Company.

On the 10th October 1988 the Prime Minister Margaret Thatcher visited the Newhaven factory on the one hundredth anniversary of the founding of the company. She is seen here signing the visitors book with, of course, a Parker Duofold Centennial pen.

One hundred years later the outstanding event in the U.K.'s Centenary celebrations was the visit of the Prime Minister, the Right Honourable Margaret Thatcher.

The visit took place on Monday, 10th October 1988 at the new headquarters of Parker Pen Limited Newhaven.

It was an inspiring visit by the Prime Minister, who following a very detailed tour around the factory and offices, gave a speech to all the staff in the main canteen. After she had cut the Centennial cake she presented long service awards to ten of the Newhaven staff who between them had accumulated 434 years of service with Parker Pen.

The speech, which the Prime Minister gave to the Parker Pen staff at Newhaven is shown below in its entirety.

"Firstly, I congratulate Parker on its Centenary. It is a great occasion. It is very good to know that, of the hundred years, sixty of them have been in Britain. I was thrilled when I read the story of the Company. For me it was always a great ambition to have a Parker Pen when I was young, and it still is my habit to sign with one...

I notice that you had a management buy out from the United States Company. I notice too that, whereas the Company under its other ownership was making a loss, you have turned it round by making a really good profit. I know the effort that went into that. **I know that you have to have superb design, superb manufacturing, excellent marketing, excellent administration and, above all, the greatest possible co-operation and spirit among all the people who work here.** *You have got it all. I am just as delighted as you are that you are now working for a company which –*

through your efforts - makes a pretty good profit, because everyone wants to know that they are doing well. That is one of the signs of success. It also means that there is a great future because, if you are making a profit, there is plenty to plough back to invest for the future - and that too you are doing. There is another very special reason why I should be pleased that you make a profit - it gives the Chancellor of the Exchequer something to tax ... So, long may you go on making an even larger profit, employing more people and winning greater market share worldwide. It is wonderful now that Parker is British. Once again we can say 'British is Best'.

It was an immense privilege for me to be able to present those long service certificates, particularly when it comes to 47 years service - because I have only done 30, so there is hope for me yet! I am also very pleased that the history of this Company is such that Winston Churchill used Parker pens. President Reagan and Mr Gorbachev used Parker pens to sign the great Intermediate Nuclear Weapon Reduction Treaty, a Treaty achieved in our time, a Treaty that I think Britain had something to do with .. . You really have had part of the history of this country running through your pens.

It has been fascinating to go round. **You have got the latest technology the latest engineering, the latest designs, and you are not only right up front, you are ahead of the rest.** *May you stay ahead of the rest. My best*

A very happy group waiting to take a personal photograph of the Prime Minister.

wishes to you for the future, for the coming hundred years - and many congratulations on all your efforts to date".

The speech was a fitting end to a momentous decade in the history of the Parker Pen Company, and a thoroughly deserved tribute to all the Newhaven staff who had contributed so much during the 1980s which, as forecast, had certainly been a decade of change.

Some of those who had received long service awards from the Prime Minister.

January 1989 and these long serving men retire with a combined total of 125 years service between them. In the photograph Vic and Betty Turner, Mick and Phyllis Evans and George and Pearl Okines.

Determination marks the faces of Parker's brave representatives in the Eastbourne Fun Run (left to right): Trevor Hatchett, Mike Thomas, Don Allaway, Penny Kemp, Cathy Eising, Jim Haggerty, Bill Young, Tom Sulley. Parker's fun runners raised £500 for charity when they ran the Eastbourne Fun Run.

Parker sponsorship helped the Newhaven Searchlight building fund to recoup more than £2,000. The event was held at the Brighton Greyhound Stadium and was supported by local companies and the stadium management.

The Duofold Desk Set.

This photograph highlights the impressive detail of the deeply sculptured engraving on the Duofold clip and the fine engraving on the pen nib.

CHAPTER 10

The 1990s and Beyond

After all the changes and excitement of the 1980s the Newhaven site continued to consolidate its position as the Headquarters of the Parker Pen Company. Even the address was changed to Parker House.

In 1991 a new prestigious office complex was built in order to accommodate Distribution, UK Sales and Marketing Divisions under one roof for the first time.

When opening the new offices on May 15th, Jacques Margry made the following remarks:

"Last year I promised our Sales and Marketing Division that if they reached certain results I would be able to justify the necessary finances to build new offices. I am delighted to tell you that these results have been achieved."

Jacques Margry, Chief Executive, shown with the two Marketing Directors Brian Robertson and Jim Haggerty. Jacques had just officially opened the newly built marketing suite in Newhaven.

Product Development which included Product Design and a newly equipped Model Shop was another area expanded to meet the constant quest for new, exciting products, accessories and packaging. These enhanced facilities serviced not only the UK but also the rest of the Parker world.

Under the direction of David Allcock several new products were launched in the early nineties all designed in Newhaven. Both the Sonnet range and the Penman accessories were manufactured in Newhaven, but the Insignia range, which had been designed in Newhaven, was produced in Arrow Park.

The very successful launch of these new Parker Pen products into the market place was a further indication that Parker was continuing to maintain its successful strategy of going 'up market'.

It also indicated that the 'centralisation' of worldwide Product Design into Newhaven was working as intended.

Parker's success in fact had been recognised in 1990 when Parker Pen UK was voted "Best Stationery Supplier of the Year" by the Link Trade Association.

Early Retirement

In February 1991 fifteen members of Parker's Newhaven staff took up the option of taking early retirement.

Les Simmons and Pony Eager both look very happy at their retirement party in February 1991. Pony had recorded 47 years of service with Valentine and Parker Pen.

Many had served virtually the whole of their working lives at the Newhaven factory.

Longest serving was Pony Eager with 47 years, closely followed by Cyril Pryer with 46 years and both Robin Tookey and Ron Pellett recorded 44 years.

In total the fifteen retirees

who included Jim Bell, Peter Blaber, Brian Cowles, Jimmy Eager, Fred Hayward, Mavis Manners, Tony Ockenden, Les Simmons, John Wells, Ted Whitfield and Charlie Winser had collectively served a remarkable 460 years.

Children in Need Appeal

The BBC Children in Need Appeal for 1990 went down as a milestone in Newhaven's history. Not only was an unprecedented amount of £11,450 raised and donated to the appeal, but a tremendous team spirit was generated amongst all of the staff. Factory, Office and Engineering and all levels of management staff played their part without any lines of demarcation.

This was the 'show stopper' - Nothing like a Dame - a parody of South Pacific presented by Parker people for the 1990 Children in Need Appeal.

The culmination of the Newhaven appeal was "The Show" held at the Meridian Centre, Peacehaven and was a complete sell out.

A cast "recruited" from all departments in Newhaven numbered over fifty. Most of these volunteers had never been on stage before, let alone having the experience of having had singing or dancing lessons - but they all performed superbly.

One of the highlights was without doubt the performance of "Nothing Like a Dame" which literally bought the house down!

The whole show was a real credit to all.

Jack King MBE

On January 16th 1992 the death of Jack King was sadly announced, he was 84.

Even after his retirement from his role as Chairman of Parker Pen UK in 1986 he still took an enormous amount of interest in the Newhaven factory.

He had joined Felix Macauley in 1923, as an Apprentice Gold Nib Maker, worked his way through the ranks, retired as Managing Director in 1972 and was then invited to serve as Chairman of the UK Board. He filled the role as Chairman for 14 years with undiminished enthusiasm for the Parker brand.

His service to the Newhaven factory therefore totalled a staggering 63 years. Jack's guiding philosophies were very simple but robust "Achieve real quality in everything you do. That is what has put the company where it is today- out in front".

His absolute insistence on quality certainly moulded a positive culture in Newhaven and one which has been consistently carried forward in spite of many changes.

For those who knew him he will always be remembered with honour and affection.

John Major at No. 10 Downing Street when he was Chancellor of the Exchequer writing with a blue Parker Duofold Centennial Fountain Pen.

Spring 1993 - Gillette

In the Spring of 1993 the Parker Pen company was acquired by the Gillette Company of Boston USA. Gillette already owned Waterman, Papermate and Liquid Paper within its Stationery Products Division, so the Parker brand was a natural addition to this division.

The news that Parker was "up for sale" first appeared in the Sunday Telegraph on Sunday 2nd February 1992. There was real concern with the staff at Newhaven who were obviously oblivious to what had been going on behind the scenes.

This prompted Jacques Margry to hold a series of meetings with all the Newhaven staff and publish a statement in the new House Magazine "Link".

What Jacques said was:

"It was unfortunate that the requirements of the City Confidentiality Agreement prevented any prior announcement or explanation - particularly as some of the local media misunderstood the message and assumed jobs were at risk.

The news is in fact the next logical step in what has proved to be a significant success story. In 1985 the Writing Instrument Group had made unacceptable losses for several years under the previous management.

When the UK Managers spearheaded the Management Buy Out, money had to be raised in the City, more specifically with the Venture Capitalists as the risks were deemed too high for conventional sources of finance.

Although the Venture Capitalists own the majority of the shares, they

Parker's marathon threesome - Bill Young, Debbie Page and Harold Napper show their medals having completed the 1991 London Marathon.

This is a photograph of an owl christened 'Parker' who somehow managed to find a perch inside the Distribution Centre. He seemed disinclined to leave his warm abode but was eventually very humanely captured and moved to a bird sanctuary at Charleston Manor where he retained the name 'Parker'.

never intended to be the permanent shareholders.

From the beginning it was foreseen that there would come a time when they would want to realise their investment. That time is now, and indeed six years is a remarkably long time for Venture Capitalists to remain with a company.

We are therefore looking for more permanent shareholders.

Selected companies throughout the world, who have the vision and

Nurses for the day! This delightful group of 'Parker Nurses' were collecting for the Rocking Horse Appeal launched for the Royal Alexander Hospital for Sick Children, Brighton. The nurses, left to right were Vicky Holman, Michelle Lee, Pat Pirie, Lucy Tucknott, Julie Havard, Amanda Stuart, Kathy Mockford and Yvette Knight.

Newhaven, Dieppe and Parker Pen commemorated the 50th anniversary of the raid, operation Jubilee, which was carried out on August 19th 1942 on the port of Dieppe. The troops, who were mainly Canadian were stationed in Newhaven. To mark the occasion a suitably engraved Parker Pen Desk Set was presented to the Mayor of Dieppe M. Christian Cuvilliez.

resources to invest in the Parker brand will be approached. A permanent shareholding will give everyone at Parker more security and will enable Parker to invest more effectively in the Market Place."

George Parker was understood to have said "I will never understand how a Group of European Managers could turn Parkers from loss to profit in such a relatively short time, when we in the USA had invested millions of dollars in an attempt to do the same and failed".

Once the acquisition was completed and Gillette was in total control, it was obvious that there would be many significant Management changes in the Newhaven based operations.

For example all of the Buy-out Directors after the 'handover' was complete had to leave the company. Peter Bentley, who had previously been in charge of the American Arrow Park operation, was given responsibility for Newhaven with the title of President Parker SBU (SBU standing for Strategic Business Unit). He in turn reported to "Chip" Hanafee President of SPG (Stationery Products Group) North America.

'The Pen is Mightier than the Sword'. Presidents Bush and Yeltsin after signing the historic arms reduction accord in Washington on 17th June 1992. Naturally they used Parker Pens to sign the accord, which they exchanged with one another after the signing.

There was also a certain amount of "decentralisation" at Newhaven with the Product Development and Product Design Operations moving to Gillette, Boston.

Gillette also moved some of its own Managers to Newhaven, particularly in the Personnel Department which in today's terminology is called Human Resources.

In 1996 the factory in Meru France was closed and integrated with the Waterman plant in Nantes. Then in 1999 the Janesville Operation at Arrow Park closed. The Frontier range and refill products were shifted to Newhaven.

An overview of the Newhaven Operation was presented in the new in-house magazine "InSite" in its No. 1 issue in Spring 1996. This is shown below:

The Newhaven Distribution Centre ships to over 70 countries and in 1995 despatched over 30 million Parker writing instruments plus accessories, nearly 40 million PaperMate writing instruments plus accessories, over 2 million Liquid Paper products and over 300,000 Waterman products plus accessories. The Service

Michelle Smith has just completed her five year Electronic Apprenticeship at Parker Pen. She is shown with a write test machine she has modified to improve its capabilities.

The end of Bays 1-9! Some of those who had spent considerable time working in Bays 1-9 are shown the site where the bays used to be.

Centre, which is also here, handles enquiries and repairs for Parker and Waterman brands within the UK and Europe.

Newhaven Manufacturing produces seven product ranges from Duofold to Jotter - 1300 different products. In addition, over 55 million Refills and nearly 3 million bottles of Quink are produced every year. This requires about 180 million pressings to be produced per annum from our Deep Draw and Bruderer Departments, over 200 million moulded items and approximately 8 million nibs. Our high volume ranges of Vector and Jotter assemble at a rate of 2/3000 units per hour.

The operation is supported by our Toolroom, Maintenance and Technical Departments which service and build new equipment and tooling

Business to Business customises about 5 million units per annum with 15 million colour applications. Also offered are chemical etching, laser engraving and many other alternative processes which personalise our products.

UK Commercial Operations sells to over 4000 customers in the UK. Its top 20 customers account for about half of the business. Customers include retail stores, other businesses using writing instruments for promotions, and office supply stores. The European Distributor Group sells to more than 20 customers in 12 different countries. There are some 770 regular employees at the Newhaven site.

There was also a very busy social calendar for the workforce. Peter Bentley introduced a Summer Fun Day, something which had been such a success at the Arrow Park factory.

The first Fun Day in July 1996 included a factory tour where the staff could invite their families to see where they actually worked. This included retirees who all received an open invitation for the

Myrtle Foard and her husband obviously enjoying the Gillette SPG Dinner and Dance in 1999.

whole day. Around 1,500 people attended in what was a most successful day. After the factory tour there was a free B.B.Q., marching bands, face painting and all sorts of activities and side shows for the children.

The Fun Day was continued very successfully for the next few years.

Another very popular introduction was the annual Dinner and Dance for all employees and partners held in January at one of the top Brighton Hotels. It was a great way for the Management to say thank you to all members of the Gillette SPG.

The helpers who made the Parker Children's Christmas Party in 1998 such as success.

Summer Fun Day in 1999 and one of the teams - 'The Yellows' who took part in the 'It's a Knockout' competition.

Football matches were also arranged between Newhaven and Waterman in Nantes on a home and away basis. Also cricket matches were played at Isleworth against Gillette.

In between all this round of socialising increased numbers of products were being successfully manufactured and more importantly sold.

Refreshing Parker

The year 2000 heralded in a new Millennium and with it a brand new Parker.

A host of new products, a new logo, new graphics and completely new packaging which was to create a refreshed and regenerated Parker.

Out went the much loved Duck Egg logo with the Parker arrow and in came a very stylish and modern $\oint$

New products launched during 2000 were a range of new high technology refills, the Reflex Range which introduced a patented soft grip, plus the Inflection and Ellipse ranges.

The Millennium year was to say the least exceptionally busy and then along came Sanford!

Sanford Take Over

In August 2000 the Gillette Company divested their Stationery Products Division to Newell Rubbermaid whose own Stationery Division, Sanford became the largest in the world,

To commemorate the Millennium, 2000, Parker produced the special Duofold Greenwich Pen shown in the photograph.

owning brands such as Rotring, Sharpie, Reynolds, Parker, Papermate and Waterman.

Again this came as a real shock to the Newhaven factory where the shop floor had no inkling that Gillette had any plans to divest its Stationery Products Division.

Gillette had spent significant sums of money in new products, re-branding and capital investment in the seven years it had owned Parker, so the plant at Newhaven was now in particularly good shape.

Sanford quickly shifted some of its other product lines, such as Rotring and Berol into Newhaven which gave more work for the factory to assimilate.

In October 2002 a specialist limited edition of the Parker 51 Fountain Pen which had been produced in Newhaven, was launched in London.

Parker introduced a whole range of new packaging plus a new logo in 2000. This photograph shows a new blister card.

The launch was hosted by

Sir Terence Conran and Denis Terrien, President of Sanford Europe, which reflected the importance placed on this particular product.

So a new era was developing on the Newhaven site where many millions of pens have been produced during the last eighty years.

Eighty years in which a few ex-Army wooden huts of the First World War have been developed into probably the world's largest and most technically advanced pen factory - and long may this success continue.

In 2002 Newell Rubbermaid who had purchased the Gillette Stationery Group moved their Sanford Stationery Division into the Newhaven factory. This of course accounts for the new company sign at the entrance to the factory.

On October 16th 2002 a special edition of the world famous '51' Fountain Pen was launched in London. It was the first '51' Pen to be manufactured for nearly 30 years.

APPENDIX I

Cronology

1921   Felix Macauley established the first Pen Factory at Newhaven.

1930   Harben Valentine purchased the Felix Macauley Pen Factory and set up the Valentine Pen Company.

1941   Parker Pen U.K. establishes "an interest" in the Valentine Pen Company in order to utilise some of its manufacturing capacity to produce Parker Pens.

1945   Parker Pen finalised the total purchase of the Valentine Pen Company.

1948   The Dover Factory opened as a "satellite" to Newhaven.

1968   Dover closed and all operations moved to Newhaven.

1982   The Parker Pen U.K. Headquarters in Grosvenor Gardens, London, closed.

1985   Parker Pen Newhaven inaugurated as the new area office for Parker Europe, Africa and the Middle East.

1986   The Management Buy-out took place resulting in the worldwide writing instrument rights being transferred to Newhaven.

1988   Parker Pen Centennial year

1993   Parker Pen sold to Gillette Stationery Products division who already owned Waterman, Liquid Paper and Papermate.

2000   Gillette disposed of their Stationery Products Division. The company is under the new ownership of Newell Rubbermaid, within their stationery division Sanford. This is now the largest stationery company in the world owning such brand names as Rotring, Reynolds, Sharpie, Waterman, Papermate, Berol and Parker.

About the Author

Malcolm Troak a local man joined Parker Pen in the Autumn of 1953,having completed his two years National Service with the Royal Sussex Regiment.

His first job with Parker Pen was working as a Toolmaker in the Toolroom,but over the years he "rose through the ranks" and eventually retired as Group Manufacturing Director in 1993.

He has therefore been in an admirable position during those forty years to have witnessed first hand most of the more significant changes within the Parker Pen organisation at Newhaven.

Malcolm has always had a very keen and active interest in both local and military history,and since his retirement from Parker Pen has written and published four books on local subjects.

He and his wife Brenda still live in East Sussex as do his three children and eight grandchildren.

Further copies are available from;

Malcolm Troak
30,Central Avenue,Telscombe Cliffs,East Sussex BN10 7LY
Tel: 01273 584009.

ISBN 0-9539115-4-3